T0328001

TOPOLOGY OF VIOLENCE

UNTIMELY MEDITATIONS

TOPOLOGY OF VIOLENCE

BYUNG-CHUL HAN

TRANSLATED BY AMANDA DEMARCO

THE MIT PRESS
CAMBRIDGE, MASSACHUSETTS
LONDON, ENGLAND

Originally published as *Topologie der Gewalt* in the series *Batterien Neue Folge* by Matthes & Seitz Berlin: © Matthes & Seitz Berlin Verlagsgesellschaft mbH, Berlin 2011. All rights reserved.

This book was set in PF Din Text Pro by Toppan Best-set Premedia Limited. Printed and bound in the United States of America.

Library of Congress Cataloging-in-Publication Data

Names: Han, Byung-Chul, author. | DeMarco, Amanda, translator.
Title: Topology of violence / Byung-Chul Han ; translated by Amanda DeMarco.
Other titles: Topologie der Gewalt. English
Description: Cambridge, MA : MIT Press, [2017] | Series: Untimely meditations |
    Translation of: Topologie der Gewalt. | Includes bibliographical references.
Identifiers: LCCN 2017026378 | ISBN 9780262534956 (pbk. : alk. paper)
Subjects: LCSH: Violence. | Power (Social sciences)
Classification: LCC HM886 .H34513 2017 | DDC 303.6--dc23 LC record available at https://lccn.loc.gov/2017026378

10   9   8   7   6   5   4

CONTENTS

Introduction

There are things that don't disappear. Violence is one of them. Modernity is not distinguished by an aversion to violence.[1] Violence is simply protean. It varies its outward form according to the social constellation at hand. Today it is shifting from the visible to the invisible, from the frontal to the viral, from brute force to mediated force, from the real to the virtual, from the physical to the psychological, from the negative to the positive, withdrawing into the subcutaneous, subcommunicative, capillary and neuronal space, creating the false impression that it has disappeared. It becomes completely invisible at the moment it merges with its opposite, that is, with freedom. Martial violence is currently giving way to an anonymized, desubjectified, systemic violence that conceals itself as such because it becomes one with society.

The Topology of Violence first addresses the *macrophysical* manifestations of violence, which take the form of *negativity*, developing in the relationship of tension between *self* and *other*, *interior* and *exterior*, *friend* and *enemy*. Typically these manifestations reveal themselves as expressive, explosive, massive, and martial. They include the archaic violence of sacrifice and blood, the mythical violence of jealous and vengeful gods, the sovereign's deadly violence, the violence of torture, the bloodless violence of the gas chamber, and the viral violence of terrorism. But macro-physical violence can also take a more subtle form, expressing itself as verbal violence, for example. Like physical violence, the violence of hurtful language is still based on negativity, since it is de-famatory, dis-crediting, de-grading, or dis-avowing. The violence of negativity differs from the violence of positivity, which arises from the spamification of language, excessive communication and information, and the accumulation of language, communication, and information.

Today's society increasingly divests itself of the negativity of the other or the foreign. The process of globalization accelerates the dissolution of borders and distinctions. Yet the depletion of negativity should not be equated with the disappearance of violence, since along with the violence of negativity there is a violence of positivity, which is wielded without enmity or domination. Violence isn't merely an excess of negativity; it can also be an excess of positivity, the *accumulation of the positive*, which manifests as over-achievement, overproduction, overcommunication, hyper-attention, and hyperactivity. The violence of positivity is possibly even more disastrous than that of negativity because it is neither visible nor evident, and it evades immunological defense because of its positivity. Infection, invasion, and infiltration—which are characteristic of the violence of negativity—now give way to infarction.

The late modern achievement-subject is free, in that it does not encounter repression on the part of sovereign entities external to itself. But in reality it is just as unfree as the obedience-subject. Once exterior repression is over-come, pressure builds within. Thus, the achievement-subject develops depression. The violence persists unabated. It merely shifts to the interior. The stages of the topological transformation of violence are *decapitation* in the sover-eignty society, *deformation* in the disciplinary society, and *depression* in the achievement society. Violence is increas-ingly internalized, psychologized, and thus rendered invisi-ble. More and more, it rids itself of the negativity of the other or the enemy, becoming self-referential.

TOPOLOGY OF VIOLENCE

I

THE MACRO-PHYSICS OF VIOLENCE

1. THE TOPOLOGY OF VIOLENCE

The Greeks called torture ἀνάγκαι. Ἀναγαῖος means "necessary" or "indispensable." Torture was perceived and tolerated like fate or a law of nature (ἀνάγκη). Here we have a society that sanctioned physical violence as a means to an end. It was a society of blood, distinct from the modern society of the psyche. In it, conflicts were resolved directly through the use of violence; that is, resolution was en*forced*. External violence unburdens the psyche because it externalizes suffering. The psyche doesn't antagonize itself with endless internal discussion. In modernity, violence assumes a psychic, psychologized, internalized form. It takes on intrapsychic forms. Destructive energies are not directly, affectively discharged but rather *worked* through psychically.

Greek mythology is drenched in blood and strewn with dismembered bodies. For the gods, violence is a self-evident, even natural, means of achieving their goals and asserting their wills. Thus Boreas, the god of the north wind, justifies his violent course of action to woo Orithyia: "So Boreas ... tried / To win by pleading, and accomplished nothing / With all his gentleness; then his natural manner, / Rough anger, rose up in him, the wind of the north, / And he growled and blustered: 'This is what I get, / What I deserve! I have thrown down my weapons / Fierceness and violence and angry spirit / Fine things to exchange for prayers! What use are they / To me? How unbecoming! Violence / Is my right weapon. ...'"[1] Ancient Greece was also a culture of fervor. It is characterized by intense emotions that take on violent form. The boar that kills the beautiful youth Adonis with its tusks embodies the violence inherent in this culture of fervor and emotion. After Adonis died, the boar is supposed to have said that it in no way wanted to injure him with its "eroticized teeth" (ἐρωτικοὺς ὀδόντας) but rather simply wanted to caress him. This paradox would ultimately be the ruin of the culture of emotion and drives.

In premodernity, violence was ubiquitous, and above all both mundane and visible. It was a significant component of social practice and communication. Thus it was not merely wielded but also expressly put on display. Rulers exhibited their power through deadly violence, through blood. The theater of brutality that was staged in public spaces also demonstrated the ruler's power and magnificence. In this context, violence and its theatrical staging contribute significantly to the wielding of power and domination.

In Roman antiquity, *munera* meant service performed for the public good. A *munus* is also a gift that is expected of someone occupying an official post. One of the *munera* is the *munus gladiatorium*. The gladiator battle itself makes up only a part of the *munus gladiatorium*.[2] Far more brutal than these battles were the midday executions that preceded them. Along with *damnatio ad gladium* (death by sword) and *damnatio ad flammas* (death by fire), there was also *damnatio ad bestias*. Criminals were thrown to hungry predators, to be mangled alive. The *munus gladiatorium* wasn't merely entertainment for the masses, intended to satisfy their aggressive drives. Rather, it exhibited an inherent political significance. In the theater of brutality, the power of the sovereign stages itself as the power of the sword. Thus the *munus gladiatorium* was an important component of the imperial cult. The ostentatious staging of deadly violence demonstrated the ruler's power and magnificence. The ruling order employed the symbolism of blood. Brute violence functioned as an insignium of power. In this context, violence did not conceal itself. It was visible and manifest. It had no shame. It was neither silent nor naked but rather eloquent and signifying. In archaic culture as well as in antiquity, the staging of violence was an integral, even central component of societal communication.

In modernity, brute violence was delegitimized not only on the political stage but also in nearly all other social milieus. It has lost virtually every *show*-place. Executions now take place in spaces to which the general public has no access. Deadly violence is no longer placed on display. The concentration camp is also an expression of this topological change. It is no showplace for execution because it isn't located in the center but rather at the *edge of a city*. The theater of bloody violence, which characterizes the society of sovereignty, yields to a bloodless gas chamber withdrawn from public view. Rather than staging its magnificence, violence conceals itself in *shame*. It continues to be wielded, but not publicly staged. It does not expressly draw attention to itself. It lacks all language and symbolism. It heralds nothing. It takes place as a mute annihilation. *Muslim* is a slang term from concentration camps referring to a victim of violence, a violence that has already become shameful, is perceived as a crime, and that renounces itself. Following its delegitimation, the sovereign's deadly violence exits the public sphere as a *place*. The camp is a *non-place*. In this sense it is different from the prison, which still is part of a *place*.

The end of the premodern society of sovereignty as the society of blood subjected violence to a topological transformation. No longer did it form a part of political and societal communication. It withdrew into subcommunicative, subcutaneous, capillary spaces within the psyche. It shifted from the visible to the invisible, from the direct to the discreet, from the physical to the psychic, from the martial to the medial, and from the frontal to the viral. Its mode of operation was no longer confrontation but contamination, not open assault but concealed infection. This structural change in violence increasingly determines its occurrence today. Terrorism doesn't focus its destructive powers frontally either but rather disseminates them virally in order to operate invisibly. And cyberwar, the war form of the twenty-first century, also operates virally. The viral nature of violence renders it invisible and nonpublic. The perpetrators make themselves invisible. Digital viruses, which infect rather than attack, leave hardly any traces that might point to the perpetrator. And yet this viral violence is a violence of *negativity*. The tension between perpetrator and victim, good and evil, or friend and enemy is still inscribed within it.

Psychological internalization is one of the central topological shifts of violence in modernity. Violence occurs in the form of a conflict within the psyche. Destructive tensions are borne internally rather than discharged externally. The front is no longer located outside the ego but within it: "Civilization, therefore, obtains mastery over the individual's dangerous desire for aggression by weakening and disarming it and by setting up an agency within him to watch over it, like a garrison in a conquered city."[3] In the conscience, Freud saw this intrapsychic surveillance entity. It is a place where violence is inverted: "We have even committed the heresy of explaining the origin of human conscience by some such 'turning inward' of the aggressive impulse."[4] Aggression against others reverses into aggression against the self. The more a person contains aggression against others, the more strict and coercive the conscience becomes.[5]

The internalization of violence also proves useful to the exercise of rule. It ensures that the obedience-subject internalizes the external ruling authority, making it a part of itself. This allows the authority to rule with far less effort. Symbolic violence is also a violence that makes use of the mechanism of habit. It inscribes itself within the things that are taken for granted, in habitual patterns of perception and of behavior. Violence is *naturalized*, as it were. Without the effort of physical, martial violence, it ensures that the established ruling relationship is maintained. The psychological internalization of force also serves disciplinary ends. By way of subtle, discreet interventions, it infiltrates the subject's neural paths and muscle fibers, subjugating it to outside ortho- and neurocorrective compulsions and imperatives.

The wholesale violence of *decapitation,* which prevails in the society of sovereignty, yields to the violence of successive, subcutaneous *deformation.*

The late modern achievement-subject is subjugated by no one. It is no longer a subject in whom subjugation (subject to, *sujét à*) is still inherent. It positivizes itself, freeing itself into a *project.* But the *transformation from subject to project* does not cause violence to disappear. Self-compulsion takes the place of outside compulsion, pretending to be freedom. This development is closely correlated with capitalist relations of production. Once a certain level of production has been reached, self-exploitation is much more efficient and productive than external exploitation because it is accompanied by a sense of freedom. The society of achievement is a society of self-exploitation. The achievement-subject exploits itself until it is completely *burned out.* In the process, it develops auto-aggressive tendencies, which often intensify to the violence of suicide. The project proves to be a *projectile,* one the achievement-subject now aims at itself.

2. THE ARCHEOLOGY OF VIOLENCE

The intractability of violence prompted Freud to deduce the existence of the death drive, which generates destructive impulses. They circulate until they discharge onto an object. By contrast, René Girard tries to avoid this hypostatization of violence by tracing it back to "mimetic rivalry." It arises because we imitate the desires of others. Things accumulate value, according to Girard's theory, for the simple reason that many people want them at the same time. We want to possess precisely what everyone else wants to possess. "Possession" mimesis provokes violent conflict. Two desires focused on the same object reciprocally hinder each other. Thus Girard infers that mimesis necessarily leads to conflict.[6] He proclaims "mimetic rivalry" to be the main source of interpersonal violence. The prohibition of mimesis, which he believed was present in many cultures, is thus a violence-preventing measure, since "any mimetic reproduction suggests violence."[7]

Girard's concept of mimetic rivalry does not capture the essence of violence, however. Etymologically, the word "rivals" can be traced to the use of waterways (*rivus*). A rival does not desire water because others desire it. Acts of violence occur above all in conflicts over things whose value does not owe to mimetic desire but rather is intrinsic. These are things that satisfy primary needs. Girard's mimesis theory also fails when it comes to money. We don't desire it because others desire it. It isn't mimetic desire that lends it value. Money is a special object because it *is* value. Mimesis represents an important form of human behavior. Without it, no socialization is possible. But it primarily concerns the symbolic, such as patterns of speech or behavior, meaning that it isn't necessarily the cause of violent conflict.

Girard also attributes revenge to mimesis. "Mimetic crisis" is his name for the deadly spiral of vengeful violence: "At the level of the blood feud, in fact, there is always only one act, murder, which is performed in the same way for the same reasons, in vengeful imitation of the preceding murder. And this imitation propagates itself by degrees. ... In such cases, in its perfection and paroxysm mimesis becomes a chain reaction of vengeance. ..."[8] The spiral of murderous violence is not caused by people imitating each other.[9] Nor does mimesis explain the destructive spiral of violence in a blood feud. Archaic revenge practice amounts to killing as such, not the imitation of killing. Killing has an *intrinsic* value. It is not a mimetic but a *capitalistic* principle that controls the archaic economy of violence. The more violence a person carried out, the more power he accumulated. Violence carried out against the other increased the actor's ability to survive. One overcame death by killing. One killed in the belief that one could thereby usurp death. This archaic economy of violence was still active in antiquity. Achilles avenges the death of his friend Patroclus by indiscriminately killing and ordering killings. Not only enemies are killed. After everyone has circled the corpse with vows of revenge, they slaughter vast numbers of cattle, sheep, goats, and pigs on Patroclus's pyre. The object is killing as such.[10] Mimesis has nothing to do with it.

Violence is, after all, the first religious experience. The all-destroying forces of nature and the murderous violence of predatory animals must have been traumatizing and frightening yet simultaneously fascinating for prehistoric people, causing them to personify those forces and animals as deities or exalt them to a superhuman reality. The first reaction to violence is its externalization. In archaic culture, there were no "forces of nature" whose intranatural causes were known, therefore rendering them unfrightening. Intra-societal violence was also consistently interpreted as a consequence of violence invading society from the outside. Nor were illness and death *intrabodily* phenomena. Rather, they were traced back to violent external influences. Every death was violent. There was neither "natural death" nor "forces of nature."

Archaic religion is a complex of interactions with violence externalized into a deity. Sacrifice represents one of the most important forms of this interaction. The Aztecs even waged ritualized wars in order to take prisoners, who would then be offered as sacrifices to the bloodthirsty god of war. The campaign was led by priests, making the war itself a sort of divine service. In this case, both war and mass killing are a sort of religious act. In archaic culture, violence represented an important medium for religious communication. Accordingly, one communicated with the god of violence *in the medium* of violence. Various relationships are possible to violence that is experienced as divine. It cannot be reduced to defense and prevention, as Girard explains it: "In primitive societies the risk of unleashed violence is so great and the cure so problematic that the emphasis naturally falls on prevention. The preventive measures naturally fall within the domain of religion, where they can on occasion assume a violent character."[11] Consequently, religious practice above all aims to placate violence, and to inhibit its unleashing, by *means* of violence, no less. The conciliatory victim was laden with all of a society's violent tendencies, which were then diverted to the exterior with the victim's death. Sacrifice is "a deliberate act of collective substitution performed at the expense of the victim and absorbing all the internal tensions, feuds, and rivalries pent up within the community. ... The purpose of the sacrifice is to restore harmony to the community, to reinforce the social fabric."[12] The victim functions as a lightning rod. Violence is diverted to a surrogate object by way of subterfuge.[13]

Again and again, Girard emphasizes that the prevention of violence is the essence of religion.[14] Undoubtedly, sacrifice also serves to prevent violence, but the religious cannot be reduced to this function.[15] The religious practice of violence isn't merely reactive and preventative; it is active and productive. If a society identifies with its god of violence or war, it will behave aggressively and violently. Thus the Aztecs waged war in the name of the violent god of war. They actively produced violence. The violence had a heightening, exalting effect. Nietzsche writes: "A nation that still believes in itself holds fast to its own god. ... [I]t projects its joy in itself, its feeling of power into a being. ... What would be the value of a god who knew nothing of anger, revenge, envy, scorn, cunning, violence? who had perhaps never experienced the rapturous *ardeurs* of victory and of destruction?"[16] The countless skulls adorning Aztec temples do not speak the language of violence prevention but rather that of active violence production. The skulls of the sacrificed are heaped on a wooden frame; their accumulation is like that of capital. The deadly violence generates a feeling of growth, of strength, of power, even of immortality. Archaic society behaved not only in an immunological-preventative manner toward violence[17] but also in a capitalist manner.

In the archaic world, every death was interpreted as the consequence of a violent external influence. One tried to avert this deadly violence, which swooped in, by countering it with an opposing violence. One protected oneself from violence by actively wielding violence. One killed in order not to be killed oneself. Killing protected against death. The more violent one became, the more invulnerable one felt. Violence functioned as a thanatological technique to survive the menace of death.

Exerting violence increased one's sense of power. More violence meant more power. In archaic culture, power did not yet represent a ruling *relationship*. It produced neither ruler nor subject. Rather, it was hypostasized to a supernatural, unpersonified substance that could be possessed, accumulated, or lost. *Mana* is what indigenous people on the Marquesas Islands call this mysterious power substance, which leapt from the victim to the victor and which a brave warrior could accumulate in great quantities: "The warrior was thought to embody the mana of all those whom he had killed. ... The mana of the warrior's spear was likewise increased with each death it inflicted. ... [W]ith a view to absorbing directly his mana, he ate some of his flesh; and to bind the presence of the empowering influence in battle ... he wore as a part of his war dress some physical relic of his vanquished foe—a bone, a dried hand, sometimes a whole skull."[18]

Viewing violence as a supernatural, impersonal means of power also casts blood feuds in a completely different light. They are no longer a retaliation against *those responsible* for the murder. No *person* is held *responsible* in this case. It also doesn't place the perpetrator in a context of *guilt*. The archaic blood feud was *undirected*, and that is what made it so devastating. The deaths suffered weakened the group to whom those killed belonged. In turn, they too had to kill, in order to restore their damaged sense of power. It didn't matter *who* was killed, only that someone was killed. Every death, even natural death, provoked vengeance. And so one killed indiscriminately. Every death generated an increase in power. It was precisely this magical economy of violence, which evades all rational logic, that made a blood feud so destructive. It even came to pass that the avenger didn't just kill members of the perpetrator's group but also bystanders who happened to cross his path. Only killing could offset the loss of power caused by the death.

The archaic form of power takes effect suddenly, like a magical substance. Power was first a substance and only later developed into a hierarchical relationship. Owing to its immediacy, this power-as-substance did not establish domination, because the latter is a complex structure of mediation and reflection. Archaic society did not display any pronounced hierarchical structure, the essence of a ruling order. Thus the leader was not a power holder as such but merely a medium: "From the chief's mouth spring not the words that would sanction the relationship of command-obedience, but the discourse of society itself about itself, a discourse through which it proclaims itself an indivisible community. ..."[19] Possessing mana, which distinguished the leader, did not make him a godlike *sovereign*. Rather, he had to constantly worry about being killed once he lost his mana.[20]

Punishment rationalizes revenge and inhibits the avalanche-like surge that makes it so destructive. In archaic society, the only possible reaction to violence was counterviolence. A radical paradigm shift separates the system of punishment from the system of revenge. It turns violence into an *action* attributable to a *person*. No longer is it an impersonal event, to be met with counterviolence. Released from the context of power, it is placed in a context of guilt. In this context, violence does not make me *powerful* but rather *guilty*. Punishment is not counterviolence, it is not revenge that the state exacts on my behalf. Instead, the objective context of guilt makes it seem just or reasonable. Thus no spiral of violence begins. The violence of punishment sheds the injustice that is characteristic of archaic revenge and that removes it from all control. Discipline and direction are mutually dependent. The system of punishment does not follow the logic of revenge but rather that of mediation, which emerges from an objective context of law. Thus it prevents the uncontrollable surging of violence since, unlike the system of revenge, it is designed not to produce but rather to prevent violence.

Pierre Clastres opposes the widespread opinion that war in archaic society was primarily an existential struggle that arose from the scarcity of vital resources, countering it with a theory that war is based solely on aggression. Contrary to Lévi-Strauss's correlation of war and exchange, he takes independent destructive energy as the basis for war, unrelated to commerce and exchange.[21] According to Clastres, archaic society was one of relative self-sufficiency, so that war need not have been waged because of scarce resources. War served only to defend the autonomy and identity of the group against others: "For all local groups, all Others are Foreigners: the figure of the Foreigner confirms, for every given group, the conviction of its identity as an autonomous We. That is, the state of war is permanent. ..."[22] Constant war creates a "centrifugal force," which generates a world of multiples, which work against unity or unification. It prevents—and this is Clastres's both central and very problematic thesis—the formation of the state. He assumes that archaic society *consciously* rejected the state, that it constantly waged war *in order* to prevent the formation of a state. As a "society against the State," archaic society was a "society-for-war." Clastres writes provocatively: "... if enemies did not exist, they would have to be invented."[23] The state is a complex *power* structure. He presupposes that power is a hierarchical relationship of domination, which, however, archaic society did not possess because of the structure of its consciousness.[24]

The archaic economy of violence didn't simply disappear in modern times. The nuclear arms race also conforms to the archaic economy of violence. The potential for destruction is built up like mana to create the impression of more power and invulnerability. At a deep psychological level, the archaic belief persists that the accumulation of the ability to kill will ward off death. More deadly violence is interpreted as less death. The economy of capital also displays a notable similarity to the archaic economy of violence. Instead of blood, it makes money flow forth. There is an essential proximity between blood and money. Capital behaves like modern mana. The more of it you have, the more powerful, invulnerable, and even immortal you consider yourself to be. Even the etymology of the German word for money, *Geld*, points to the context of sacrifice and cult. Thus it's presumed that money was initially a medium of exchange with which sacrificial animals could be obtained. If someone had a lot of money, it meant that he could have many sacrificial animals, which could be offered up at any time. The owner also possessed an enormous, predator-like deadly violence.[25] Money or capital is thus an instrument against death.

On a deep psychological level, capitalism actually has much to do with death and fear of death. This is also what gives it its archaic dimension. The hysteria of accumulation and of growth and fear of death are mutually dependent. Capital can also be interpreted as time spent, since others can be paid to work in one's stead. Endless capital creates the illusion of endless time. The accumulation of capital works against death, against the absolute lack of time. Faced with a limited life span, people accumulate time as capital.

Alchemy attempts to transmute base metals into precious ones. Lead, in particular, was considered base. It was associated with Saturn, the god of time. In the Middle Ages he was often depicted as an old man with a scythe and hourglass, that is, with the symbols of impermanence and death. The alchemical transformation of lead into gold resembles the attempt to conjure away time and impermanence in favor of endlessness and immortality. The *aurum potabile* promised eternal youth. Overcoming death is the essence of the *alchemical imagination*, and it also feeds the capitalist economy, with its hysteria for growth and accumulation. The stock market, in this sense, is the *vas mirabile* of modern capitalism.

The sacred economy also follows the logic of accumulation. For Calvinists, economic success alone could generate the *certitudo salutis*, the certainty of being among the elect who would escape eternal damnation. Endless savings equal salvation. Anxieties surrounding salvation, which accompany fear of death, trigger the capitalist compulsion for accumulation. One invests in and speculates on salvation. There is an analogy between the archaic economy of mana, the capitalist economy of capital, and the Christian economy of salvation. They are all thanatological techniques for abolishing death, *spiriting it away*.

The capitalist economy absolutizes *survival*. It is not concerned with the *good* life.[26] It feeds on the illusion that more capital generates more life, and more ability to live. The rigid, rigorous separation of life and death suffuses life itself with a ghostly rigidity. Concern for the good life yields to hysteria for survival. The reduction of life to vital biological processes strips life itself bare. Mere survival is obscene.

It robs life of its *liveliness*, which is much more complex than mere vitality and health. The mania for health arises where life has become bare, like a piece of currency, and void of any narrative content. Faced with the atomization of society and the erosion of the social, all that is left is the *body of the self*, which must be kept healthy at all costs. The loss of ideals leaves the attention-desperate self with only *exhibition value* and *health value*. Bare life wipes out every teleology, every in-order-to, which would provide the purpose for being healthy. Health becomes self-referential and hollows out into *functionality without function*.

Life has never been so fleeting as it is today. Nothing promises permanence or perpetuity. In the face of a lack of being, nervousness arises. Hyperactivity and acceleration of the process of life are an attempt to counteract the emptiness in which death announces itself. A society dominated by the hysteria for survival is a society of the undead, capable neither of living nor of dying. Freud was also aware of this fatal dialectic of survival when he closed his essay "Reflections on War and Death" with the aphorism "*Si vis vitam, para mortem*," that is, "If you wish life, prepare for death."[27] The idea is to grant death more space in life to prevent life from stiffening into undeath: "Were it not better to give death the place to which it is entitled both in reality and in our thoughts and to reveal a little more of our unconscious attitude towards death which up to now we have so carefully suppressed? This may not appear a very high achievement and in some respects rather a step backwards, a kind of regression, but at least it has the advantage of taking the truth into account a little more and of making life more bearable again."[28]

3. THE PSYCHE OF VIOLENCE

Freud's psychic apparatus is a system of negativity. The superego manifests as an authority with strict commands and prohibitions: "The superego retains the character of the father, while the more complex the Oedipus complex was and the more rapidly it succumbed to repression (under the influence of discipline, religious teaching, schooling, and reading), the more exacting later on is the domination of the superego over the ego—in the form of conscience or perhaps of an unconscious sense of guilt."[29] The superego expresses itself as a "categorical imperative" with the "harshness and cruelty exhibited by the ideal—its dictatorial 'Thou shalt,'"[30] with a "harshly restraining, cruelly prohibiting quality." It "rages against the ego with merciless fury. ..."[31] Its main modal verb, *should,* makes the ego an obedience-subject: "As the child was once under the compulsion to obey its parents, so the ego submits to the categorical imperative of its super-ego."[32] The superego is an internalized, controlling entity that stands for god, the sovereign, or the father. It is the *other* within the self. As such, violence here is a violence of negativity, as it issues from the *other*. It expresses itself as repression in a rulership context.

Resistance, negation, and repression organize Freud's psychic apparatus as a system of negativity. It is constantly wracked by the antagonistic tensions of instinctual impulses and their repression. The unconscious also owes its presence to repression. According to Freud, the unconscious and repression are correlated to a "very great extent."[33] The instinctual representative "proliferates in the dark, as it were, and takes on extreme forms of expression," which become destructive. Symptoms of hysteria or obsessive-compulsive disorder can in large part be tied to violence that is active in the psychic apparatus. It is like an arena in which operations such as defense, occupation, retreating, pulling back, camouflage, invasion, and infiltration take place. The ego, the id, and the superego ultimately behave like a military encampment, forming a clear *front*. They do occasionally declare peace, but it is based on unstable power relations.

Throughout, Freud keeps to the pattern of negativity when he describes psychological processes. Thus he constantly follows the tracks of the other, which eludes appropriation by the ego. Accordingly, the healing of mental illness consists in a complete appropriation of the id by the ego. He also traces melancholia back to the other, which nests within the ego, changing it. Like mourning, melancholia arises from the renunciation of a beloved object. Unlike mourning and the grieving process, which pull the libido away from the lost object to cathect[34] its new object, in melancholia the object is internalized. Because of the weak cathectic energy, the object is easily given up, but the newly freed libido does not cathect another object. Rather, a narcissistic identification with the object arises: "An object-choice, an attachment of the libido to a particular person, had at one time existed; then, owing to a real slight or disappointment coming from this loved person, the object-relationship was shattered. The result was not the normal one of a withdrawal of the libido from this object and a displacement of it onto a new one. ... The object-cathexis proved to have little power of resistance and was brought to an end. But the free libido was not displaced onto another object; it was withdrawn into the ego. There, however, it was not employed in any unspecified way but served to establish an *identification* of the ego with the abandoned object. ... In this way ... the conflict between the ego and the loved person [was transformed] into a cleavage between the critical activity of the ego and the ego as altered by iden- tification."[35] The abandoned object, to which the ego had an ambivalent relationship, is internalized as part of the ego. The critique of the relinquished object, that is, the other, becomes a critique of the self. In reality, the self-reproach and self-abasement are intended for the other, which has now become a part of the ego. Melancholia lies at the heart of a division within the ego. A part of the ego opposes the other, criticizing and belittling it: "In melancholia the occa- sions which give rise to the illness extend for the most part beyond the clear case of a loss by death, and include all those situations of being slighted, neglected or disap- pointed, which can import opposed feelings of love and hate into the relationship or reinforce an already existing ambiv- alence. ... If the love for the object ... takes refuge in narcis- sistic identification, then the hate comes into operation on this substitutive object, abusing it, debasing it, making it suffer and deriving sadistic satisfaction from its suffering."[36] Identification with the object transforms sadism into masochism. By way of self-punishment and self-torment, the ego revenges itself upon its original object.

The question of whether Freud interpreted melancholia correctly is not particularly important to us here. Only his explanatory model as such carries weight. Melancholia is a pathologically disturbed relation to the self. Freud interprets it as an external relationship, a relationship to the *other*. The violence that the melancholic does to him- or herself is thus a violence of negativity since it is directed at the *other within the ego*. The *other within me* is the formulation of the negativity that consistently organizes Freud's psychoanalysis.

Freud's psychic apparatus is a repressive apparatus of domination and compulsion that operates with commands and prohibitions, that subjugates and oppresses. Just like disciplinary society, it is full of walls, barriers, thresholds, cells, borders, and border posts. Freud's psychoanalysis is therefore possible only in repressive societies, such as the society of sovereignty or the disciplinary society, which base their organization on the negativity of prohibitions and commands. But today's society is a society of achievement, one that increasingly rids itself of the negativity of prohibitions and commands, presenting itself as a society of freedom. The modal verb that dominates the society of achievement isn't the Freudian "should" but rather *can*. This societal shift entails restructuring within the psyche. The late modern achievement-subject possesses a *completely different psyche* than the obedience-subject to whom Freud's psychoanalysis refers. Freud's psychic apparatus is dominated by negation and repression, and by fear of transgression. The ego is the "abode of anxiety."[37] The *big Other* causes its anxiety. The late modern achievement-subject is poor in negation. It is a subject of affirmation. If the unconscious were necessarily associated with the negativity of negation and repression, the late modern achievement-subject wouldn't have an unconscious anymore. It would be a post-Freudian ego. The Freudian unconscious is not a timeless entity. It is the product of the negativity of prohibitions and the repression of the restrained disciplinary society, which we, however, have long left behind us.

The work performed by the Freudian ego consists above all in fulfilling a duty. That is a point of similarity with the Kantian obedience-subject. In Kant, the conscience takes on the position of the superego. His moral subject is also exposed to the *violence* of an *authority* (both words are *Gewalt* in German): "Every human being has a conscience and finds himself observed, threatened, and, in general, kept in awe (respect coupled with fear) by an internal judge; and this authority watching over the law in him is not something that he himself (voluntarily) *makes*, but something incorporated into his being."[38] The Kantian subject is also divided. It works at the behest of the other, which, however, is a part of itself: "Now, this original intellectual and (since it is the thought of duty) moral predisposition called *conscience* is peculiar in that, although its business is a business of a human being with himself, one constrained by his reason sees himself constrained to carry it on as at the bidding *of another person*."[39] As a result of this division, Kant speaks of the "doubled self" or of a "dual personality."[40] The moral subject is at once the defendant and the judge.

The obedience-subject is not a subject of desire but rather of duty. Thus the Kantian subject also goes about its duties and represses its "inclinations." However, Kant's god, this "supreme moral being," appears not only as an authority of punishment and judgment but also as one of *gratification*. Though as subjects of duty, moral subjects repress all pleasurable activities in favor of virtue, the moral god *rewards* their work, performed under the condition of suffering, with happiness. Happiness is "distributed in exact proportion to morality."[41] The moral subject, who suffers pain for the sake of morality, is completely assured of gratification. No crisis of gratification looms here because God doesn't deceive; he can be depended on.

Late modern achievement-subjects don't pursue any obligatory work. Their maxims are not obedience, law, and the fulfillment of duty but freedom, desire, and inclination. Above all, they expect to reap pleasure from their work. They do not act at the behest of others. Rather, they listen mainly to *themselves*. Their job is to be their own boss. Thus they divest themselves of the negativity of the *demanding other*. However, this freedom from the other isn't just emancipating and freeing. The dialectic of freedom entails the development of new constrictions. Freedom from the other becomes a narcissistic relationship to the self, which is responsible for many of the achievement-subject's psychic disorders.

The lack of relationship to the other causes a crisis in gratification. Gratification as recognition assumes the authority of the other or a third party. It is not possible to reward or recognize yourself. For Kant, God is the authority of gratification. He rewards and recognizes moral achievement. Because of the disturbed structure of gratification, the achievement-subject feels compelled to achieve more and more. The lack of relationship to the other is also the *transcendental* condition for the possibility of the crisis of gratification. Today's relations of production are also responsible for this gratification crisis. It is no longer possible to view an achievement as the result of *completed, finalized* work. Today's relations of production prohibit *closure*. Rather, one's work is *open-ended*. We lack forms of closure, which have a beginning and an end.

Richard Sennett also traces the crisis of gratification back to a narcissistic disorder and the lack of relationship to the other: "As a character disorder, narcissism is the very opposite of strong self-love. Self-absorption does not produce gratification, it produces injury to the self; erasing the line between self and other means that nothing new, nothing 'other,' ever enters the self; it is devoured and transformed until one thinks one can see oneself in the other—and then it becomes meaningless. ... The narcissist is not hungry for experiences, he is hungry for Experience, looking always for an expression or reflection of himself in

Experience. ... One drowns in the self. ..."[42] In experiences, one encounters the *other*. One changes and becomes *other*. Experience, on the other hand, extends the ego into the other, into the world. Thus it draws on *resemblance*, on sameness. Self-love is thus still determined by negativity, as it devalues and repels the other in favor of the self. The self *opposes* the other. It is asserted by demarcating itself from others. To love oneself is to position oneself expressly against the other. In the case of Narcissus, on the other hand, the border with the other blurs entirely. Those who suffer from a narcissistic disorder sink into themselves. If any point of reference to the other is completely lost, no stable conception of the self can form.

Sennett is correct to link the modern individual's psychic disturbances with narcissism, but he comes to the wrong conclusions: "Continual escalation of expectations so that present behavior is never fulfilling is a lack of 'closure.' The sense of having reached a goal is avoided because the experiences would then be objectified; they would have a shape, a form, and so exist independently of oneself. ... The self is real only if it is continuous; it is continuous only if one practices self-denial. When closure does occur, experience seems detached from the self, and so the person seems threatened with a loss. Thus the quality of a narcissistic impulse is that it must be a continual subjective state."[43] According to Sennett, the narcissistic individual *intentionally* avoids reaching a goal because an objectifiable form can arise from closure, which persists independent of the self, thereby weakening the self. In reality, it does just the opposite. The socially determined impossibility of objectively valid, definitive forms of closure drives the subject into a narcissistic repetition of itself, never arriving at a *form*, a stable self-image, or *character*. The subject doesn't consciously "avoid" the feeling of having reached a goal in order to increase its sense of self. *Rather, the subject never has the feeling that it has reached a goal.* It's not as if the narcissistic subject doesn't *want* to reach closure. In fact, it is not able to. Out in the open, it loses itself in dissipation. This lack of closure is to a large extent economically necessitated; after all, openness and open-endedness facilitate growth.

Hysteria is a typical psychic affliction of the disciplinary society in which psychoanalysis developed. It presumes the *negativity* of repression, prohibition, and negation, which lead to the formation of the unconscious. The instinctual representatives [*Triebrepräsentanz*] shunted into the unconscious manifest by means of "conversion" as physical symptoms that unambiguously mark the sufferer. Hysterics display a *characteristic* morph. Thus, unlike depression, hysteria can be described in terms of its morphology.

"Character," according to Freud, is a phenomenon of negativity, because without the censorship of the psychic apparatus, it would not take form. Thus, Freud defines it as "a precipitate of abandoned object-cathexes."[44] When the ego learns of the object-cathexes arising within the id, it either tolerates them or fends them off with repression. The history of repression is inscribed within character. It represents a certain relationship between the ego and the id, and between the ego and superego. While the hysteric displays a certain *morph*, the depressive is formless, a-*morphous*. He is a *man without character*. The hysteric's psyche may be subject to external compulsions, but in turn, it is in some measure orderly and formed. A psychic apparatus that has become depressive may be free of the negativity of repression and negation, but it is chaotic, disordered, and formless.

Freud's psychoanalysis presumes the negativity of repression and negation. As Freud emphasizes, the unconscious and repression are correlated "to a very great extent." No process of repression and negation is involved in modern-day psychic afflictions such as depression, burnout, and ADHD, in contrast. Actually, they point to an *excess of positivity*: not to negation but rather to the inability to *say no*, not to that which *isn't allowed* but to the *ability to do everything*. Thus psychoanalysis cannot broach them. Depression doesn't result from repression on the part of controlling entities such as the superego. In depressives, this "transference"—which would provide indirect clues to repressed psychic content—doesn't occur.

With its ideas of freedom and deregulation, present-day achievement society is abolishing wholesale those barriers and prohibitions that characterized the disciplinary society. The abolition of negativity bolsters performance. A general limitlessness and dissolution of barriers ensues, a veritable state of *general promiscuity*, which exerts no repressive energy. Where the release of instinctual impulses is not hindered by restrictive sexual mores, paranoid delusions also do not occur, such as those suffered by Daniel Paul Schreber, which Freud traced back to his repressed homosexuality. The Schreber case is typical of the nineteenth-century disciplinary society, where a strict prohibition of homosexuality and even desire prevailed.

The unconscious is not responsible for depression. It no longer governs the depressive achievement-subject's psychic apparatus. But Alain Ehrenberg evidently adheres to its significance, which warps his argumentation: "The history of depression has helped us ... understand this social and mental turnaround. Its irresistible rise permeates the two pairs of changes that have affected the individual in the first half of the twentieth century: (1) psychic liberation and identity insecurity and (2) individual initiative and the inability to act. These two pairings display the anthropological risks at play in the movement from neurotic conflict to depressive inadequacy in the field of psychiatry. The individual emerges from the battle to face messages from this unknown person she cannot control, this irreducible part that Westerners call the unconscious."[45] Depression symbolizes the "irreducible" that "cannot be controlled," according to Ehrenberg.[46] It arises from "confrontation between the notion of limitless possibility and the notion of the uncontrolled."[47] Accordingly, depression occurs when the subject founders on the uncontrolled and struggles for initiative. The uncontrolled, the irreducible, and the unknown are like the unconscious figures of negativity, which are no longer constitutive of the society of achievement, with its excess of positivity.

Freud understands melancholia as a destructive relationship to the other that is internalized as part of the self through narcissistic identification. The original conflict with the other is internalized and transformed into an adversarial relationship to the self, which leads to impoverishment of the ego and auto-aggression. The contemporary achievement-subject's depression is not preceded by an adversarial, ambivalent relationship to the other, which is lost. The *dimension of the other* plays no part in it. Instead, its strained, overdriven, excessive self-reference takes on a destructive character, contributing to the depression in which burnout so often culminates. The exhausted, depressive achievement-subject wears itself down, so to speak. It is tired, exhausted by itself, by the war with itself. Completely incapable of stepping outside itself, of being *outside*, of depending on the *other* or on the world, it becomes engrossed in itself, which paradoxically leads to the hollowing out and emptying of the self. It commits itself to an ever-accelerating hamster wheel *within itself*.

New media and communications technology also attenuate *being toward the other*. The virtual world is poor in otherness and its resistance. In virtual spaces, the ego can basically operate without the "reality principle," which would provide a *principle of the other and of resistance*. In these *imaginary* virtual spaces, the narcissistic ego mainly encounters itself. Virtualization and digitization are increasingly contributing to the disappearance of the real, which is notable above all for the resistance it provides. Reality causes us to *hold on*, both in the sense of pause and grasp.

Not only does it interrupt or resist, it also provides support and a foothold.

The late modern achievement-subject has a surfeit of options at its disposal but is not capable of forming an *intensive bond*. In depression, all bonds break, even bonds with the self. Mourning differs from depression primarily in its strong libidinous bond to an object. Depression, in contrast, has no object and is therefore not *directed*. It also makes sense to differentiate depression from melancholia. Melancholia is preceded by an experience of loss. Thus it always exists *in a relationship*, namely, *in a negative relationship to the absent*. Depression, on the other hand, is cut off from all relationships and bonds. It lacks all *gravity*.

Mourning occurs when an object with a strong libidinal cathexis is lost. Someone who mourns is completely with the beloved *other*. The late modern self expends most of its libidinous energy on itself. What is left of the libido is spread thin across steadily increasing contacts and fleeting relationships. It's very easy to withdraw the very weak libido from the other, cathecting new objects with it. The tedious, painful "grieving process" proves completely unnecessary. "Friends" in social networks primarily fulfill the function of heightening the narcissistic sense of self by paying attention like consumers to the *ego on display* like a product.

Alain Ehrenberg supposes that there is a merely quantitative difference between melancholia and depression. Melancholia, which has an elitist ring to it, is democratized as depression today: "If melancholia was the domain of the exceptional human being, then depression is the manifestation of the *democratization of the exceptional.*"[48] Depression is "melancholia plus equality, the perfect disorder of the democratic human being."[49] However, Ehrenberg specifically locates depression in the era in which sovereign man, whose arrival was heralded by Nietzsche, became a widespread reality. That makes the depressive someone who is "exhausted by his sovereignty" and who no longer has the strength to master himself. He is worn out by the constant "need for initiative." Ehrenberg contradicts himself in his peculiar etiology of depression: melancholia, which already existed in antiquity, cannot be derived from the sovereignty that characterizes the modern or late modern individual. The melancholic person of antiquity is anything but a depressive who lacks the strength to be "master of himself" or "passion for being oneself." Like hysteria or mourning, melancholia is a phenomenon of negativity, while depression owes to an excess of positivity. But can we perhaps detect a congruity between depression and democracy? According to Carl Schmitt, depression is characteristic of democracy to the extent that it lacks *definitive power of decision.* The *violence of decision* cuts cleanly, preventing protracted conflict from occurring. In this light, depression is not marked by "the decline of conflict as a reference point" but rather by the lack of reference to an *objective deciding entity,* which would produce forms of closure[50] and provide gratification.

Ehrenberg takes stock of depression solely with an eye to the psychology and pathology of the self, failing to take the economic context into account. Burnout, which often precedes depression, is less an attribute of that sovereign individual losing the strength to be "master of himself." Rather, burnout is the pathological consequence of *voluntary* self-exploitation. The imperative to personal expansion, transformation, and reinvention, which is the flip side of depression, presumes a wide array of products associated with identity. The more one changes identity, the more dynamic these products become. Industrial disciplinary society relies on unchanging identity, while the postindustrial society of achievement requires flexible people to ramp up production.

Ehrenberg's thesis is that "the success of depression lies in the *decline of conflict as a reference point* upon which the nineteenth-century notion of the self was founded."[51] For Ehrenberg, conflict fulfills a constructive function. According to him, both personal and social identity form from elements that are "in relationship because of their conflict."[52] In political as in private life, conflict forms the normative core of democratic culture.[53] But depression masks the difficulty with which relation arises from conflict. Thus, conflict no longer endows people with their unity.

This model of conflict dominates classical psychoanalysis. Healing consists in *recognizing*, that is, in becoming conscious, that an intrapsychic conflict is present. However, this model of conflict presumes the negativity of repression and negation. Thus it cannot be applied to depression, which is completely lacking in negativity. Ehrenberg may recognize that depression is characterized by a lack of relationship to conflict, but he stands steadfastly by his conflict model. According to Ehrenberg, a hidden conflict lies at the root of depression. Antidepressants only make the user dependent while concealing the conflict further. Conflict, he says, is no longer a "reliable guide": "Deficit filled, apathy stimulated, impulses regulated, compulsion tamed—all of this has made dependency the flip side of depression. With the gospel of personal development on the one hand and the cult of performance on the other, conflict does not disappear; however, it loses its obvious quality and can no longer be counted on to guide us."[54] In reality, depression completely eludes the conflict model, that is, psychoanalysis. Ehrenberg attempts to rescue psychoanalysis even *after its conditions have ceased to exist*.

The "deconflictualization" that Ehrenberg associates with depression must be considered in the context of the general *positivization of society*, which brings with it a de-ideologization of society. Social-political events are no longer determined by the now archaic-sounding *struggle* between ideologies or classes. But the positivization of society has not eliminated violence. Violence originates not only in the negativity of conflict but also in the positivity of consensus. The *totality of capital*, which now appears to be absorbing everything, represents a *consensual violence*.

The fact that today clashes occur not between groups, ideologies, or classes but rather between individuals is not so pivotal to the crisis of the achievement society as Ehrenberg would believe. What is problematic is not so much individual competition itself but rather its self-referentiality, which exacerbates it into *absolute competition*. The achievement-subject competes with itself, falling victim to the destructive compulsion to outdo itself. Here, performance is not determined *in relation* to others. The point is no longer to outdo and defeat others. The struggle is with the self. But the attempt to defeat and outdo oneself has deadly consequences. Competition with the self is fatal, like *trying to chase your own shadow*.

In the transition from the disciplinary society to the achievement society, the superego positivizes itself into the *ego ideal*. The superego is repressive. It mainly voices prohibitions. It dominates the ego with the "harshness and cruelty exhibited by ... its dictatorial 'Thou shalt,'" with its "harshly restraining, cruelly prohibiting quality." The achievement-subject *bases itself* on the ego ideal, while the obedience-subject *debases itself* before the superego. These are two different modes of being. The superego generates negative compulsions. In contrast, the ego ideal exerts positive compulsions on the ego. The negativity of the superego constrains the ego. Basing the self on the ego ideal, on the other hand, is interpreted as an act of freedom. But in the face of the unattainable ego ideal, the self sees itself as deficient, a loser to be assailed with self-reproach. Auto-aggression develops out of the gap between the real ego and the ego ideal.[55] The ego struggles with itself, is at war with itself. The society of positivity, which believes it has freed itself from all external compulsions, entraps itself in destructive self-compulsions. Psychic ailments such as burnout or depression, the exemplary ailments of the twenty-first century, all exhibit auto-aggressive tendencies.

One does violence to oneself and exploits oneself. External violence is replaced by self-generated violence, which is more devastating because its victims imagine themselves to be free.

4.   THE POLITICS OF VIOLENCE

4.1.   FRIEND AND ENEMY

According to Carl Schmitt, differentiating between friend and foe is the essence of the political.[56] Political thought and political instinct are nothing more than the "ability to distinguish friend and enemy."[57] "Friend/enemy" isn't the usual binarism, which makes the political system different from other systems. It isn't just one system among many, or merely another "domain." The "domain" of the moral—you could call it a "system"—is determined by the antithetical dyad "good/evil." And the opposition of "beautiful/ugly" defines the system of aesthetics. But politics isn't a subject area. The "friend/enemy" distinction is therefore something fundamentally different from the antitheses that construct a domain or social system. A domain and its antitheses merely register the facts. "Beautiful" and "good" are predicates of an object. A person can also be beautiful or good. But, as Schmitt would argue, those are *factual* attributes. The antitheses friend and enemy, on the other hand, are not differentiated factually but rather *existentially*. An enemy need not be morally evil or aesthetically ugly. A factual opposition "denotes the utmost degree of intensity of a union or separation, of an association or dissociation"[58] in order to represent the existential binary "friend/enemy." Thus the moral distinction between good and evil can reach the political dimension only by means of *existentialization*. Like aesthetics and morality, religion and economics are primarily just factual domains. They depend on factual distinctions. But as soon as a religious community wages war for its convictions, that is, battles an enemy, it is acting politically: "The real friend-and-enemy grouping is existentially so strong and decisive that the nonpolitical antithesis, at precisely the moment at which it becomes political, pushes aside and subordinates its hitherto purely religious, purely economic, purely critical criteria and motives to the conditions and conclusions of the political situation at hand." Existentialization deprives the factual domain of its factuality, lending it irrational tendencies. Thus, according to Schmitt, there is no *war based on facts*.

For Schmitt, a community only becomes political when an enemy poses an existential threat and it must assert itself—that is, in war. The real possibility of violence is the essence of the political. The battle occurs not only between states but also within a state. A state is also internally political when faced with an internal enemy. According to Schmitt, this is why the "declaration of an internal enemy"[59]—known in the legal system of the Greek republic as the *polemios* declaration and in Roman law as the *hostis* declaration—exists in all states, enforced through ostracism, banishment, proscription, and proclamations deeming the wrongdoer *hors-la-loi* or *sacratio*.

The existential opposition of friend and enemy "suffices" to mark the genuinely political, Schmitt emphasizes, and to differentiate it from "mere societal-associational groupings."[60] Like Heidegger, Schmitt distinguishes community from society. Only communities develop political energy. Society, on the other hand, is just an "association." It lacks the will, the interiority, and the determination to struggle, indeed determination with regard to itself. An economically organized society may be able to lay waste to its opponents by "nonviolent" means. But that still doesn't make it a political unit because its opponent isn't an "enemy," just a "competitor." For Schmitt, war isn't merely politics by other means but rather the *political itself*.

He believes that enmity is constitutive of identity. The *ego* owes *its existence* only to its immunological defense against the other as enemy. Thus Schmitt remarks that it is a "sign of inner conflict to have more than one real enemy." The inability to clearly define a single enemy is interpreted as a lack of identity on the part of the self. The plurality of enemies dissipates the ego. Only in the face of *an* enemy does the self manifest in complete clarity and distinctness: "The enemy is our own question as *Gestalt*. ... For this reason I must contend with him in battle, in order to assure my own standard, my own limits, my own Gestalt."[61]

The high-water mark of great politics for Schmitt isn't the moments in which reconciliation or rapprochement is achieved but rather those moments in which "the enemy is, in concrete clarity, recognized as the enemy."[62] It is not dialogue and compromise but war and strife that form the foundation of the political: "What always matters is only the possibility of conflict."[63] The solution to conflicts is not political; rather, the enmity that lies at the heart of conflict establishes the political. The "possibility of conflict"[64] is not the borderline case marking the end of the true political. Instead, as a *front*, the *border* defines the space of the political. The exceptional case is one in which all of a society's normative conditions are invalidated.[65] They are reduced to their bare being. The normative yields completely to the existential. The political manifests itself in this critical exception, in which *existence* finds its pure expression: "War, the readiness of combatants to die, the physical killing of human beings who belong on the side of the enemy—all of this has no normative meaning, only an existential meaning, particularly in a real combat situation with a real enemy."[66] Thus no normative justification of war is possible, only an existential one. Indeed, there can be no *justi*fication for war. The norms establish the "normal situation."[67] Only a "critical," "entirely abnormal situation" in which norms no longer apply can be called political. Schmitt severs war from any kind of normativity: "The justification of war does not reside in its being fought for ideals or norms of justice, but in its being fought against a real enemy."[68]

To Schmitt, the political is not work. In fact, it feeds on the tension of the incalculable. You might say that "calculation"—management, administration—lacks all existential tension. "Society" dissipates a "politically united people" into a merely "culturally interested public." Schmitt's concept of the political as a form of *Dasein* is reminiscent of

Heidegger's jargon of authenticity. Heidegger's the "they" ("*Man*") is completely unpolitical in Schmitt's sense, as it lacks all heroic decisiveness. Schmitt would say that the "they" isn't capable of war, only of competition. What's more, the "they" flees the *situation* in which *decisiveness* counts: "The they is everywhere, but in such a way that it has always already stolen away when Da-sein presses for a decision."[69] In "The Self-Assertion of the German University" ("*Rektoratsrede*," 1933), which Heidegger composed one year after the publication of Schmitt's *The Concept of the Political*, he also invoked a "battle community" led by "communally tuned saying."[70] *Sein*, then, is battle. Thus it gains a political dimension.

According to Schmitt, everything comes down to decision, to the decisive battle, to the *cutting violence* of decision. Decision renders discussion superfluous. *The they* discusses, Heidegger would add. Discussion lacks the power of decision [*EntscheidungsGewalt*], the decisive blow that marks decision. For this reason, Schmitt only speaks disparagingly about discussion: "Thus the political concept of battle in liberal thought becomes ... discussion. ... Instead of a clear distinction ... there appears the dynamic of perpetual competition and perpetual discussion."[71] As is well known, Schmitt is a staunch opponent of parliamentarianism. The word "parliament" derives from the French verb *parler*. From this vantage point, speaking with one another and discussion are the essence of the political. Dictatorship does without discussion. It reduces speech to command. But to command is not the same as *parler*. For Schmitt, the *parliamentization of speech* would be a degeneration, the *parliamentization of the psyche*. Schmitt's psyche doesn't have patience for the expansiveness and openness of *parler*. It degrades into *palaver*, which goes on endlessly without leading to a final decision. The word "decision" derives from the Latin *decidere*, which means "to cut off." Decisions are made by grabbing the other, the enemy, and slitting his throat. One cuts off whatever the enemy is trying to say. A decision is an unmediated verdict made with the sword. It is based on *violence*. Discussion as a medium for the political follows an entirely different school of thought. *Compromettere* takes the place of *combattere*.

Schmitt thinks in terms of irreconcilable, dichotomous opposites. Either-or is the basic precept of his thought, even of his *psyche*. Stark contours articulate his world. His critique of romanticism grows from his inability to accept ambiguity and ambivalence. For him, the world of romanticism is "a world without substance and functional cohesion, without a fixed direction, without consistency and definition, without a final court of appeal."[72] He condemns the romanticist Adam Müller's "passion for mediating everywhere; his 'cosmic tolerance,'" which left nothing "that one could love and honestly hate." Schmitt criticizes "his emotional pantheism, which is basically always in agreement with everything and approves of everything," and "his feminine and vegetative nature,"[73] which stood in opposition to masculine, predatory natures. Political existence is not vegetative but bestial. Reconciliation and mediation are not political but rather aggression and subjugation. Life only achieves a "*political* factor" through "real battle," "this most extreme possibility," that is, through violence. For Schmitt, a transnational world community is not a political situation because it has no enemies outside itself: "A world in which the possibility of war is utterly eliminated, a completely pacified globe, would be a world without the distinction of friend and enemy and hence a world without politics."[74]

Schmitt's politics of violence is a *politics of identity*, which characterizes his *psyche* beyond the political. His hydrophobia also stems from his compulsion for identity. For Schmitt, water is a very frightening element because it does not permit any kind of stable delimitation. It is completely *without character* because nothing can be inscribed within it: "The *sea* knows no such apparent unity of space and law, of order and orientation. ... On the sea, ... firm lines cannot be engraved. The sea has no *character*, in the original sense of the word, which comes from the Greek *charassein*, meaning to engrave, to scratch, to imprint."[75] Schmitt is thus a true land creature in that he thinks in terms of clear decisions and dichotomies[76] and has no concept of the floating or indistinguishable.

Schmitt's politics of identity releases large amounts of destructive energy. But its violence is directed outward. It is inwardly stabilizing because all adversarial energies are conducted away from the self and thus externalized. Violence aimed at the other as enemy lends stability and persistence to the self. It is identity forming. As he notes, "The enemy is our own question as *Gestalt*." Only when faced with the enemy does the self acquire "my own standard, my own limits, my own Gestalt." In turn, *excluding* the clearly marked other as enemy forms the *conclusive,* distinct self-image. The more distinct the enemy, the more clearly contoured my *Gestalt* will be. The image of the enemy and the self are mutually dependent. The destructive energies directed at the other contribute constructively to the formation of a clearly delineated self.

"*Character*" is a phenomenon of negativity because it presupposes exclusion and negation. Thus it is a character flaw "to have more than one real enemy." It follows that it would also be a character flaw to have more than one real friend. Despite or precisely because of its negativity, character gives form to the self and stabilizes it. The violence of decision and exclusion cuts cleanly, which also lends "character" its rigor, is at odds with today's achievement society, in which it is imperative not to commit oneself to anything. The achievement-subject must be *flexible*. The reasons for this shift are primarily economic. Rigid identity hinders the acceleration of contemporary relations of production. Durability, consistency, and continuity thwart growth. The achievement-subject finds itself in a state of constant flux, with no final location and no clear self-contours. The ideal achievement-subject would be *characterless*, or actually *character-free*, available for any purpose, while the disciplinary and obedience-subject must display a consistent character. Up to a certain point, the state of flux is accompanied by a feeling of freedom. Over time, it leads to psychological exhaustion.

Orthopedic, orthopsychic repression isn't only destructive. It also gives the psyche a *form*, a *position*. The total loss of negativity deforms and destabilizes. Without any "location," the psyche can't get a handle on things. It flies off the handle and becomes underhanded. The loss of stable, verifiable models of identity and orientation results in psychic instability and *character disturbances*. The inconclusive and unconcluded nature of the self makes it not only free but also sick. One could say that the depressive achievement-subject is a *man without character*.

Present-day achievement society isn't governed by the immunological *friend/enemy* principle. As Schmitt says, a "competitor" is not an enemy. Etymologically, "compete" means to seek *together*. It is a competition for *something*. Between two enemies, what is at stake is not a thing but existence itself. A competitive relationship lacks *existential tension*, the negativity of enmity that aids in forming a clear self-image. The late modern achievement-subject increasingly rids itself of negativity. It faces neither its enemy nor its sovereign. No outside authority forces it to continually achieve more. Rather, it forces itself and wages war with itself.

The other first announces itself as resistance. A total loss of resistance would level the other to *the same*. Enmity is a relationship to the other that produces a great deal of friction. As society positivizes, the late modern individual increasingly sheds the *negativity of the other*. Its freedom emerges as freedom from the other, which becomes a pathologically heightened relationship to the self. In turn, it loses more and more of its relationship to the outside, to objects, and to the world. New media and forms of communication intensify this development. One also encounters little resistance from others in virtual space. It serves as a projection area in which the late modern individual mainly encounters itself.

The disciplinary subject and the obedience-subject are faced with the *other*, which manifests itself as God, a sovereign, or certainty. They are subjugated to an external authority, which generates repression and punishment, but also *gratification*. The subject of achievement society is characterized by narcissistic self-referentiality. Because it receives no gratification from the other, it is forced to achieve more and more. Though the negativity of the other is still present in competitive relationships, the subject lacks this negativity because, after all, it competes with itself and tries to outdo itself. It must run a devastating race, endlessly *circling itself* until it collapses.

Depression can be understood as a narcissistic disorder. It originates in the dissipating relation to the other, as well as in the lack of relation to the exterior and to the world. It threatens the narcissistic subject, which is circling itself, wound up in itself. Its agonizing occupation with itself—which, as Schmitt says, does not lead to "my own Gestalt"—can facilitate the construction of an imaginary external enemy, unburdening the psyche which had been overburdened with itself, demoralized by and at war with itself. This constructed idea of the enemy helps the self find a verifiable "*Gestalt*," which frees it from its debilitating narcissistic self-reference and pulls it from drifting in the subjective void. Modern-day xenophobia displays this imaginary dimension.

To free itself from the narcissistic hamster wheel, in which it circles *itself* ever more quickly, it would have to restore a relationship to the *other*, one beyond Schmitt's enemy/friend principle and its concomitant violence of negativity. A different construction, indeed a reconstruction of the other, is necessary, one that doesn't provoke a destructive immunological defense. It should be possible to have a relationship to the other in which I affirm it in its otherness, allowing it to be as it is. This *yes to its being* is called friendship. This friendship is not a passive, indifferent, live-and-let-live relationship with the other but rather an active, involved relationship to its being. It awakens only in the face of the other or the stranger. The more different they are from the self, the keener is the kindness extended to them. When faced with the *same*, neither friendship nor enmity is possible, neither *yes* nor *no*, neither welcome nor rejection.

The politics of friendship is more open than the politics of tolerance. Tolerance is actually a conservative practice because otherness is merely tolerated. It still maintains a stable self-image bound to a clearly defined identity. Furthermore, it strictly delineates the self from the other. Nor is the practice of tolerance free from domination. The power-holding majority allows minorities to remain. The politics of friendship generates a maximum amount of solidarity from a minimum amount of commonality, maximum nearness from minimum relation. In Schmitt's politics of violence as a politics of identity, on the contrary, even brotherhood based on a maximum of relation could transform into enmity. Schmitt answers the question, "Why is my enemy?": "The other proves to be my brother, and my brother proves to be my enemy."[77]

4.2. LAW AND VIOLENCE

It is widely assumed that a legal system loses its effectiveness when it has no violent means at its disposal with which it can enforce its agenda. That would make law nothing more than the privilege of the powerful, only enforceable through violence. The law may indeed require the possibility of violent enforcement, but it isn't necessarily *based on* it. Hegel writes: "Representational thought often imagines that the state is held together by force; but what holds it together is simply the basic sense of order which everyone possesses."[78] It is not the threat of violence or negative sanctions alone that stabilizes the legal system. Violence doesn't *stabilize* anything. It doesn't provide a stable foothold. In fact, widespread violence is a sign of internal instability. A legal system that could only be propped up with violence would be very fragile. Only compliance with the legal system can provide stability. Violence makes an appearance at the moment when "stabilizing" factors disappear completely from the legal system.

Walter Benjamin's political philosophy also infers the inner unity of violence and law. As a legislative power, violence is in effect at the origin of law. Benjamin conceived of law as the privilege of the powerful. The victors violently assert their will, their interests, even their existence. The legal relationship simply reflects the power relationship: "Lawmaking is power making."[79] Thus, violence is fundamental to lawmaking. Benjamin takes the legend of Niobe as an example of the relationship between law and violence: "True, it might appear that the action of Apollo and Artemis is only a punishment. But their violence establishes a law far more than it punishes for the infringement of one already existing. Niobe's arrogance calls down fate upon itself not because her arrogance offends against the law but because it challenges fate—to a fight in which fate must triumph, and can bring to light a law only in its triumph."[80] Violence continues to remain in effect beyond the establishment of the law. As law-preserving violence, it ensures that established law is followed by erecting a backdrop of threats. For Benjamin, the law is inseparable from violence through the entire sphere of its effect. It is *based* on violence. Violence is the *essence* of the law. Benjamin entirely ignores the mediating, violence-deterring dimension of the law, which was addressed as early as Hesiod: "... listen now to right, ceasing altogether to think of violence. / For the son of Cronos has ordained this law for men, / that fishes and beasts and winged fowls should / devour one another, for right is not in them; / but to mankind he gave right which proves / far the best."[81]

Right, the law, is subject to historical and structural change. It first manifests as an awesome, fateful power. One unsuspectingly transgresses against an unwritten law and must atone. Benjamin invokes this archaic, mythical model of law and generalizes it to the *essence* of the law. "*All* legal violence," according to Benjamin, is a "mythical manifestation of immediate violence." Because of its relationship to violence, the law is "pernicious" and unsuited to justice. Benjamin reminds us of "the perniciousness of its historical function, the destruction of which thus becomes obligatory."[82]

Benjamin's essay "Critique of Violence" was written during the Weimar Republic–era years of crisis. Like Carl Schmitt, he expresses his skepticism regarding parliamentarianism: "They lack the sense that a lawmaking violence is represented by themselves; no wonder that they cannot achieve decrees worthy of this violence but cultivate in compromise a supposedly nonviolent manner of dealing with political affairs."[83] The *essence* of the parliament apparently escapes Benjamin. It is a place for speaking with each other (*parler*). The parliament shifts the task of legislation from violence to speech. Compromise is free of brute violence as long as it is an outcome of speaking with each other. In contrast, a moment of absolute silence and speechlessness is inherent in violence. Benjamin mistakes the essence of compromise when he identifies a "mentality of violence"[84] within it. Those who truly have a mentality of violence aren't interested in compromise in the first place. Democracy has a *communicative essence*. Minorities can also definitely influence the decision-making process *by speaking*. Dictatorship prohibits speaking; it dictates.

Benjamin's critique of parliamentarianism is differently motivated than Carl Schmitt's. The latter discredited parliamentarianism in favor of a legislative decisive force or violence. Benjamin's parliamentary critique, on the other hand, follows from a radical skepticism toward the law itself. Benjamin's God is not a sovereign who makes laws. While Carl Schmitt doesn't leave the immanence of the legal system, Benjamin is focused on a legal hereafter. His basic skepticism toward the legal system originates with its genealogical and generative relationship to violence. Precisely because of the original violent nature of the law, he dismisses the concept of parliamentarianism: "... however desirable and gratifying a flourishing parliament might be by comparison, a discussion of means of political agreement that are in principle nonviolent cannot be concerned with parliamentarianism. For what parliament achieves in vital affairs can only be those legal decrees that in their origin and outcome are attended by violence."[85] Nor do legal contracts represent a nonviolent settlement of conflicts for Benjamin, because they give each party the right to apply violence should the other party break the contract. Benjamin always draws his examples of the legal relationship from liminal situations and exceptional cases, such as the case of the contract being broken. This approach completely obscures the mediating function of the law, which is the essential difference between law and violence. A contract is based on the premise that the two parties will behave as stipulated, and that they are prepared to abstain from violence and to speak with one another. Like a compromise, a contract is an *effect of speech*. Its *communicative essence* cannot be reduced to the economy of power and violence.

In light of the violent character of the law, Benjamin asks if there are any nonviolent means to manage the interests of people in conflict. First he affirms the possibility of nonviolent conflict resolution: "Without a doubt. The relationships of private persons are full of examples of this. Nonviolent agreement is possible wherever a civilized outlook allows the use of unalloyed means of agreement."[86] Benjamin contrasts "[l]egal and illegal means of every kind that are all the same violent" with "unalloyed means." They are unalloyed insofar as they are free from any sort of legal relationship. He counts "[c]ourtesy, sympathy, peaceableness, trust" among these nonviolent means. Trust, for example, is more informal than a contractual relationship, because it forgoes the violence of the broken contract. Where trust disappears, violence finds a way in. Benjamin draws attention to the fact that in the millennia-old history of nations, nonviolent means of agreement have emerged and are mutually implemented by diplomats to solve conflicts in a way that is analogous to agreements between private individuals, peacefully and without contracts. He even speaks of "[a] delicate task that is more robustly performed by referees, but a method of solution that in principle is above that of the referee because it is beyond all legal systems, and therefore beyond violence."[87] A "policy of pure means"[88] is an extra-ordinary one, that is, one that goes beyond the policy of compromise and mediation that derives from the legal order. Benjamin elevates language itself to the "sphere of human agreement," "the proper sphere of 'understanding,'" which is "wholly inaccessible to violence." However, Benjamin places limits on the effectiveness of pure means. He only speaks of the "policy of pure means"[89] in connection with international conflict in which conciliation must be achieved because the involved parties fear the detriments of a violent confrontation, whatever its outcome. Benjamin's policy of pure means isn't an ethics but rather a technique of agreement that can be implemented for conflicts concerning goods: "They [the pure means] therefore never apply directly to the resolution of conflict between man and man, but only to matters concerning objects. The sphere of nonviolent means opens up in the realm of human conflicts relating to goods."[90]

Benjamin is convinced that "every conceivable solution to human problems, not to speak of deliverance from the confines of all the world-historical conditions of existence obtaining hitherto, remains impossible if violence is totally excluded in principle. ..." And so he inquires into a completely different sort of violence that has evaded all legal theory.[91] Since Benjamin rejects all human legal systems because of their connection with violence, but at the same time holds complete abstinence from violence to be impossible, he falls back on a divine violence that is "pure" insofar as it is free from any legal system or mythical legislation.

According to Benjamin, divine violence is pure because it *ruptures* the tie that binds law to violence and inter*rupts* any involvement in the legal system. Thus, it is dis*ruptive*. It does not establish relationships of power and domination. Mythical violence, in contrast, generates a guilt-based legal situation that turns the vanquished into the guilty. Guilt comes into existence when violence prevails. Thus Niobe is kept alive "as an eternally mute bearer of guilt." Her perpetuated suffering confirms the dominant mythical violence. Divine violence "expiates" because it itself *ruptures* the context of guilt. Since it is free of power and domination, it is not directing, governing, or administrative; that is, it is not "executive." Thus, Benjamin refers to it as "sovereign" violence. Law-preserving violence is also called "administrative violence." As sovereign violence, divine violence would be a violence that evades all administration, all executives and executions, all economy, all calculation, and every technique.

The Niobe myth is contrasted with God's judgment on the company of Korah: "It strikes privileged Levites, strikes them without warning, without threat, and does not stop short of annihilation. But in annihilating it also expiates, and a deep connection between the lack of bloodshed and the expiatory character of this violence is unmistakable."[92] Mythical violence is lawmaking. Moreover, it inculpates and demands atonement at once. Divine violence, on the other hand, is law-destroying and expiating. This diametrical opposition is problematic. The Niobe myth is undoubtedly about power and lawmaking. The victory of the goddess Leto ratifies her sole right, her privilege, to be honored by humans. It codifies the difference between humans and gods. Her bloody violence is lawmaking and border-defining. But divine violence does not differ fundamentally from this mythical violence. Korah revolts against Moses. God's annihilation of his tribe ratifies Moses's rule. Moses references it as justification for his rule. He *interprets* it as a sign that he is chosen, and that he is particularly close to God. The one concrete example given to exemplify pure divine violence is not actually pure. Like mythical violence, it is contaminated by domination and power. Divine violence is ultimately nothing more than an imaginary authority that can be called on by any ruling power to legitimate itself. Every retroactive interpretation and construction of meaning implicates it in mythical violence.

Benjamin lists other points of difference, which also don't quite add up. Mythical violence is bloody.[93] It is "bloody power over mere life. ..." Divine violence, in contrast, is "lethal without spilling blood." According to Benjamin, blood symbolizes life that clings to possession and power. Divine violence may be annihilating, but "only relatively, with regard to goods, right, life, and such like, never absolutely, with regard to the soul of the living."[94] The "soul" is a pure sphere that is divested of legal, power, and possessive relationships, that is, of mere life. As an impure means, the rule of law is restricted to blood, to mere life: "For with mere life the rule of law over the living ceases."[95]

But even in its "perfected" and purest form, "educative power," which "stands outside the law" and which Benjamin characterizes as pure violence, does not leave the "soul" undisturbed. There is simply no education that is free of dispositives, which are adjacent to myths. This pure form of violence is imaginary, a form that "myth bastardized with law."[96] Benjamin falls into the logic of *bastardization*, which cannot sustain deconstruction. If there were such a thing as pure violence, it couldn't *appear*. Visibility would make it subject to *interpretation*, which acts on myths and makes them impure.

Following Benjamin's path, Agamben considers law only in light of violence. This leads him to demonize it, withdrawing like Benjamin into the messianic realm of longing where "humanity will play with law just as children play with disused objects. ..."[97] According to his theory, the fundamental proximity of law and violence manifests in the state of exception in which valid law is abdicated, while the basis of its validity, that is, the legislating violence of sovereignty, announces itself. The sovereign who presides over the state of exception is "a threshold of undecidability ... at which *factum* and *ius* fade into each other."[98]

Regulation is always accomplished as spatialization and localization. Sheer violence alone is not capable of forming spaces or creating locations. It lacks the space-building force of mediation. Thus it cannot produce a legal *space*. Only power, not violence, is capable of space building. Agamben differentiates between power and violence. Violence must become power in order to establish a space. Otherwise it fizzles at the moment of its action. Violence meets with a no in the form of a negation. Power, in contrast, develops along a yes. The greater the popular approval of the ruler, the greater is the ruler's power.

The smaller the difference between the ruler's will and that of the subjects, the more stable is the ruler's power. A truly divine sovereign whose word was law would also be capable of calling forth a unified will. The sovereign's will would immediately become everyone's will. No violence would be required for lawmaking. Such a sovereign would not meet with opposing wills because they themselves would *first* generate that will. Their effect would therefore be neither disruptive nor destructive but rather purely creative. Bare violence is not capable of making law. It is ineffectual in the face of an absolute no. Even forcible subjugation contains a yes. It is always possible to counter violence with a fearless no. An absolute no negates the relationship of power, that is, subjugation. The law attains stability only by dint of an *assenting* yes. Roman dictators who were given full authority for a limited period during crises, for example to wage war, held referendums on laws to ensure the support of the people even though they were not obliged to do so, thus accumulating true power.

Politics attends to the ruling of the state (*polis*), which, according to Aristotle, "while it comes into existence for the sake of life, it exists for the good life [*eu zen*]."[99] Law and justice are essential to politics. They have a mediating effect and ensure successful coexistence, maximizing the common good. The state (*polis*) is far more than a structure of power and domination. It is not a weakness but rather the strength of Aristotle's *Politics* that it is not based on domination. The goal of the *polis* is "self-sufficiency" (*autarkeia*). People come together to form a community because alone they suffer deficiencies. A political community arises from a sense of deficiency and not from a will to power and domination. People resolve to live with others to overcome the feeling of deficiency. Politics developed for the sake of life and survival, but it's only the concern for the "good life" that makes it what it truly is.

Politics is mediation. It must mediate the legal system, and even justice itself. That is why Aristotle attached such importance to friendship. It is more mediating than law and justice. Thus Aristotle comments that good lawmakers should be more concerned with protecting friendship than with justice. Above all, friendship moderates social coexistence more efficiently, and, most important, with less violence, than the legal system. That is why the ideal *zoon politikon* must be a friend: "And if men are friends, there is no need of justice between them; whereas merely to be just is not enough—a feeling of friendship also is necessary."[100] Negotiation is political in the emphatic sense, making use of extralegal forces of mediation and compromise. The politics of friendship prevents crisis situations that would require legal arbitration from occurring in the first place. Aristotle elevates friendship to "the greatest of blessings for the state."[101] It is a symbol of the political in general, since "friendliness is an element of partnership."[102] Aristotle places friendship on a very fundamental, existential plane. Thus, friendship is the foundation of the state, the condition for its existence, for friendship is nothing less than "the motive of social life."[103] The will to rule isn't *political* in the emphatic sense, but the *motivation to live together socially* is.[104] Human life is not politicized through its relinquishment to an absolute power over death. Only the decision to live together politicizes human existence.[105] Neither power nor violence is animated by the genuinely political idea of community, that is, the motivation to live together. Power does assume a community, but it is ultimately a phenomenon of the self, that is, *ipsocentric. Togetherness* is not its intention.

Agamben allows law and violence to collapse into each other completely. He even claims that politics has been "contaminated by law."[106] Furthermore, he has recourse to Hobbes, arguing: "All representations of the originary political act as a contract or convention marking the passage from nature to the State in a discrete and definite way must be left wholly behind."[107] Agamben arrives at this claim through a distorted reading of Hobbes. Hobbes himself thinks of the political with the contract as starting point. He defines the state as "*one person*, whose will, by the compact of many men, is to be received for the will of them all; so as he may use all the power and faculties of each particular person to the maintenance of peace, and for common defence."[108] In *Leviathan*, the state is also defined as "one person, of whose acts a great multitude, by mutual covenants one with another, have made themselves every one the author, to the end he may use the strength and means of them all as he shall think expedient for their peace and common defence."[109] The subjects themselves are *authors* of all of the sovereign's acts and judgments. Thus, "whatsoever he [the sovereign] doth, can be no injury to any of his subjects. ..."[110] In the end, the subjects are subjugated only to themselves, that is, to their own wills, which are simultaneously the will of all. Those who accuse the sovereign of injustice are complaining about something whose authorship is their own responsibility. They accuse themselves. The subjects as citizens see themselves reflected in the sovereign and encounter themselves in each of his acts. This complex structure of mediation oriented toward the "common benefit" is genuinely political. The commonwealth owes its existence to the *political* motivation to *live together*. Hobbes does not refer to the sovereign's violence,[111] whose purpose it is to defend the legal system, as *violence* but rather as "*common power*." Political power originates with this *common* action according to a shared will. *Violence* is not *political*. It does not produce the legitimacy that paves the way for legality and positive norms. *Political* or *common* will is legitimizing. This "common" is what distinguishes power from violence. It defies Agamben's negativity-based model.

Problematically, Agamben consistently refers to sovereign power as "*violenza*." In doing so he erases the eminently important semantic difference between *common power* and *violence*. He reduces power to malignity and aligns it with violence. He also maligns the police. They "are perhaps the place where the proximity and the almost constitutive exchange between violence and right" is exposed.[112] Agamben collapses the police into the position of the sovereign, which can "make no distinctions between the civilian population and soldiers, as well as between the people and their criminal sovereign, thereby returning to the most archaic conditions of belligerence."[113] In Agamben's eyes, the exercise of *ius belli* during the Gulf War took on the guise of a police operation, "not obliged to respect any juridical rule."[114] Consequent on his demonization of the law, which he completely collapses into violence (*violenza*),[115] there isn't much room for political philosophy in Agamben. "Pure" politics is a politics of "communicative emptiness," which alone must signal "the *factum loquendi*," the unalloyed experience of language itself. Communicative emptiness manifests communicativity itself, communicability within the realm of communication. Agamben links *factum loquendi* with *factum pluralitatis*, the fact that humans form communities: "But because what human beings have to communicate to each other is above all a pure communicability ... politics then arises as the communicative emptiness."[116]

The society in which Benjamin and Schmitt lived was a *society of negativity*, shaped by world wars and the *immunological* paradigm of friend and enemy. Agamben, in contrast, lives in a *postimmunological* society, one that has left both the society of sovereignty and the disciplinary society behind. Despite this decisive paradigm shift, Agamben continues to think in terms of negativity, such as the state of exception or banishment. To disastrous effect, they are projected onto the society of positivity, which increasingly divests itself of all negativity. This projection makes Agamben blind to the problems of the postimmunological society. In the midst of the society of achievement, he describes the society of sovereignty. Therein lies the anachronism of his thought. Because of his anachronism, the violence he traces is always one of negativity, based on *exclusion* and *inhibition*. Thus he overlooks the violence of positivity, which expresses itself as *exhaustion* and *inclusion* and which is characteristic of the achievement society. Because he attends exclusively to the secularized forms of the now archaic-seeming forms of negativity, the *extreme phenomena of positivity* elude him. Contemporary violence is based more on the *conformity of consensus* than on the *antagonism of dissent*. Thus one could invert Habermas's phrase and speak of the *violence of consensus*.

The crisis of contemporary society is not, as Agamben claims, that the state of exception has become normalcy, boundlessly expanding the sphere of sovereignty to the point that there is no longer any difference between law and violence. Rather, the crisis is that no state of exception is possible anymore because everything is absorbed by the *immanence of the same*. The "hell of the same"[117] produces particular forms of violence beyond the violence of negativity.

Today, politics itself is positivizing itself into work without any possibility of *sovereign action*. It is positive work in that it never calls into question the forces and compulsions it is subject to, nor can it raise itself above them. The positivity of work perpetuates the normal state. Politics as work lacks any *transcendental horizon* beyond which the *merely possible* could point. Politics is immobilized in the immanent space of capital, which meanwhile has absorbed all transcendence and everything exterior to it. Because of the positivization of politics, political parties and ideologies are also increasingly losing meaning. *Political emptiness* is filled with the spectacle of media theatrics. Politicians also establish themselves in this depoliticized space of spectacle. It is not their political *acts* but rather their *personality* that is staged in the media.

Agamben is fascinated by theological figures. He sees them returning, secularized, in modernity. Thus, he believes he can establish the doxological dimension of rulership in contemporary media: "[T]he media are so important in modern democracies ... above all because they manage and dispense glory, the acclamative and doxological aspect of power that seemed to have disappeared in modernity."[118] Contemporary democracy is "entirely founded upon glory, that is, on the efficacy of acclamation, multiplied and disseminated by the media beyond all imagination."[119] Contrary to Agamben's supposition, the contemporary media inhabit a depoliticized, detheologized space of spectacle. If anything, it generates *glory without a kingdom*. Politics as work also advances without any domination or glory. *To come to light,* it cloaks itself in the medial glow of spectacle. *Political emptiness* hollows it out, creating a politics of the spectacle, which neither does, nor says, nor produces anything significant but merely communicates communicability. The politics of the spectacle is *a politics of communicative emptiness*. Thus Agamben's utopian formula of *communicability without communication* becomes the *empty formula of communication as spectacle.*

Domination and glory have long been absent from the political field, shifting to the interior of capital. Advertisements represent the capitalist version of liturgical hymns. Celebrities who praise new products are the angels of today. Capitalist hymns produce glory. It is the beautiful glow of domination, which pertains only to capital. The *acclamation* paid to capital's domination is now called *consumption.*

5. THE MACRO-LOGIC OF VIOLENCE

Macro-physical violence develops in the tension between self and other, friend and enemy, interior and exterior. The *negativity of the other* is constitutive of it. Infiltration, invasion, and infection are the forms it takes. In it, violence expresses itself as an effect that comes from the outside, attacks me, and overpowers me, robbing me of my freedom. It forces its way inside me without my consent. But not every effect from the outside is violence. When I consent to it and incorporate it into my practices, building a *relationship* to it, it is no longer violence. I behave *freely* in relation to it. I affirm it as part of the contents of myself. If this internalized appropriation is absolutely impossible, I experience it as violence. It forces its way into my interior and destroys it. If violence is incorporated into the self despite failed internalization, it forms an introjection, which nonetheless remains external. This encapsulated trauma is violence because it cannot be processed, treated, and discarded like a theme.

Violence occurs not only at the interpersonal level. Thus it makes sense to *formalize* it into a negative tension between the interior and exterior, in order to be able to register and describe this macro-physical form of violence, which cannot be constrained to the conflict-filled intermediary space between the self and the other. At that point the violence can be described as an event that prevails but cannot be internalized. It exposes the interior to an exterior that defies the interior structure of order and meaning. It expresses itself as the de-internalization of the interior by the exterior. The exterior represents both a *different* system of order and meaning and the forces that work against order as such. If the interior does not manage to establish continuity in relation to the exterior and to internalize it, the invasion of the exterior breaks it. Violence is the rift that does not allow for mediation or conciliation.

While power forms a continuum of hierarchical relationships, violence causes rifts and ruptures. The constant structural characteristic of violence is the hiatus, which differs from the hierarchy that is constitutive of power. Hierarchy is difference, a gradient within a continuum, and unlike hiatus, it is connective and binding. Power always *organizes itself* as a power structure. The structure of violence, in contrast, is an oxymoron; there is only the destruction of violence. Structure and construction are the marks of power. Violence, in contrast, is marked by rupture and corruption. Power and violence both make use of a method of bending. Power bends otherness until it bows, until it submits. Violence bends otherness until it breaks.

Violence robs its victim of any possibility of action. There is no room to maneuver. Violence annihilates space. In this sense it also differs from power, which leaves room for action. Power does not categorically preclude action and freedom. It uses the freedom of others, whereas violence crushes it. The subjects of power can even *subject* themselves to the sovereign's will. Rushing to be obedient, they make my will their own. Indeed, my will brings their will into being. Thus it is not violence and violation but leadership and misleading that gain access to the freedom of others.

Violence and power are strategies to neutralize the disturbing otherness and unruly freedom of the other. The power of the self brings about the subjugation of the other. The other gives up its otherness, which is disturbing and threatening to the self. Power enables the self to extend *itself* into the other. Power is also the ability to transform the relationship to the other into a relationship to the self, to self-reference; that is, given and even despite the other to remain with oneself. This continuity of self reduces the disturbance generated by the otherness of the other. Power is a relational word. It minimizes the otherness of the other but does not completely extinguish it. Instead, the other remains involved in the actions of the self. Unlike power, violence is not a relational word. It destroys the other.

Neither violence nor power is capable of *allowing the other to be as it is*. They are attempts to neutralize the otherness of the other. Love also lacks freedom and composure toward the other. Heidegger evidently had a different sort of love in mind when he defined it as follows: "Truly the deepest interpretation of what love is stands in the words of Augustine: 'amo volo ut sis.' I love you, which means that I want the you to be as you are. Love is allowing to be in the deepest sense, according to which it calls forth being."[120] Love is the "innermost freedom of one toward the other."[121] However, the intentionality of wanting, of *volo*, lends ambivalence and ambiguity to this love. Arendt expresses her justified suspicion: "'Volo ut sis' can mean: I want you to be how you really are, to be your essence—and that isn't love, but desire for mastery, which, under the pretense of confirming love, even wants to make the essence of the other into the object of its own will."[122] "*Non enim amas in illo quod est; sed quod vis ut sit*" ("You love in him not what he is, but what you would have him be").[123] It isn't necessarily desire for mastery if I want you to be how you really are. But this love is based primarily on the generosity of a master. It is only possible in a hierarchical relationship, between god and man or father and son, for example. Thus it is not completely free of power. It is characterized by asymmetry and verticality. Thus Augustine writes on the love of fathers for their sons: "*Puto quia, si amas filios tuos, vis illos esse; si autem illos non vis esse, non amas*" ("I suppose that if you love your children you want them to be; if, however, you do not want them to be, then you do not love them").[124] The intentionality of *volo* places love under the regime of the self. It deprives it of composed friendliness toward the other. The other is freed to *be as it is* wherever *volo* withdraws. The "innermost" freedom toward the other is still not the *utmost* freedom toward the other, which could only be achieved in *friendship*.

Love and friendship both remain under the regime of the self. Thus, according to Aristotle, a friend is "another self" (*allos autos*).[125] "[V]ery intense friendship," he says, "resembles self-regard."[126] Friendship does not transcend the regime of the self, which violence and love are also both subject to. Achilles says to Penthesilea: "True, by the power of love I am your slave, / And I shall wear these bonds forevermore; / By luck of arms, though, you belong to me; / For it was you, my precious friend, who sank / At *my* feet when we fought, not I at yours."[127]

Power is a medium for action. It functions like a lock on a canal, influencing or accelerating the action. It accelerates action because those subject to power immediately take on and carry out the decisions of the power holder. Violence, on the other hand, is not a medium for action. It can be used as an instrument to achieve a certain goal in a very direct fashion, but primarily its goal is not to steer or influence action. Since power is a medium for action, it can be applied constructively. Violence, by contrast, is inherently destructive. It is only productive or generative when it is exercised with the intention of converting it into power, of establishing power. In this case violence and power are related to each other as means and end. Violence carried out against the *being* of the other as such, however, pursues no worldly end. It exhausts itself in the act of destruction. Absolutely destructive power, on the other hand, is a contradiction. Power always possesses a constructive core. Power *works*. It organizes and develops its area of influence by producing norms, structures, and institutions, inscribing itself within a symbolic order. Unlike power, violence does not *work.* Organization and management are not its traits. Thus it is de-*structive.* Nietzsche recognized the particular intentionality of power when he differentiated it from violence: "The feeling of power first conquering, then ruling (organizing)—it regulates that which has been overcome for the benefit of *its own* preservation, and therewith preserves *that which has been overcome itself.*"[128] Power is not primarily destructive. Rather, it is "organizing." To organize is to connect and to mediate. It confines the subject of power to a space organized in accordance with power, which stabilizes the rulership and makes it enduring.

Massive resistance to the ruler arises from insufficient power. Violence is implemented because of lack of power. Exercising violence is the desperate attempt to convert powerlessness into power. A truly powerful ruler is not powerful through the incessant threat of violence. Power can of course be enforced with violence, but this sort of power is fragile. It is easily torn asunder, owing, in fact, to the rifts caused by violence. It is erroneous to assume that power is based on violence. Violence has a different intentionality than power. It is possible to conceive of a violent event that isn't a power event. Killing motivated by hate is different from violence that exhausts itself in extinguishing the being of the other. It does not want to dominate the other. If violence is viewed only in light of power, its essence is not recognizable. And if power is viewed only in light of violence, the particular intentionality of power is not visible.

Power is a *relationship* that connects the self and the other. Power functions symbolically, relating and consolidating (*sym-ballein*).[129] But power can also take on diabolic forms. Diabolic power expresses itself repressively, destructively, divisively, and exclusively. If only the diabolic side of power is taken into consideration, its highly productive symbolism disappears. Violence, on the other hand, is not a symbolic medium. Its essence is diabolic, that is, divisive (*dia-ballein*). As a result of its symbolic dimension, power can generate the many symbols that lend it its eloquence. As a result of its diabolic nature, violence is poor in symbolism and language.

An increase in power is an increase in space. Victory in war leads to acquisition of territory. An empire is a realm of empowerment. It is as large as its power will reach. The acquisition of space takes place not only on the territorial but also on the (inter)personal level. The ruler is continued in the subjects and therefore *grows* in proportion to them. The ruler's astral body is as large as the reach of their power. It is coextensive with the space over which the ruler rules, that is, which is occupied by *the ruler's self*. This topology of power explains why a ruler's total loss of power is experienced as a total loss of territory. The body of the ruler, which was as large as the ruler's sphere of power, shrinks to the size of the ruler's tiny mortal body when power is lost.

Unlike space-shaping, spatializing power, violence destroys space and leaves *emptiness* in its wake. It is depleting and de-internalizing. Power, in contrast, expresses itself as internalization and concentration. Spaces of power are spaces of language. They are saturated with symbols, signs, and meanings. To destroy a space or body of power, it must be divested of its language. Thus, in Hartmann von Aue's *Erec*, the imprisoned knight Cadoc, who embodies the courtly system of power and domination, is stripped and skinned by a giant. Power is a principle of formation, while violence destroys forms. Power achieves a certain order by establishing differences and borders. Violence, in contrast, dissolves borders. Power establishes measure. Violence opposes measured power. It is measureless. Things that are *violent* exceed measure.

Violence is always aimed at the bearer of interiority. The shattering of a stone isn't violence. Only people or communities or systems have interiority. For them, ipso-centric striving toward the *self* is inherent in *self*-settlement. As a destructive intrusion from the outside, violence is de-internalizing. It unsettles the *settled self*. That's why it sets people on edge. Settlement always implies the possibility of being un-settled. Unlike violence, power is not unsettling, because it settles things. Continuity, interiority, and settlement determine the workings of power. Discontinuity, de-internalizing, and unsettling are the constant structural markers of violence. Both macro-physical violence and power are phenomena of negativity. Of vital importance to them is the antagonistic tension of interior and exterior, what is proper to the self and what is foreign to it.

In the process of the positivization of society, power is also increasingly losing significance as a socio-immunological medium. The power of sovereignty belongs to the distant past, with its violence of decapitation. Today, political as well as economic organizations are dismantling hierarchical structures. Power is no longer a key medium of politics. Political practice increasingly rids itself of theory, drama, and ideology, dividing itself into a number of domains, which are overseen by experts and commissions. The increasing positivization of society also casts all violence, physical as well as psychic, in a reprehensible light. But that doesn't mean the end of violence, because violence doesn't only arise from the negativity of the other, but also from excessive positivity. The violence of positivity doesn't deprive, it saturates; it doesn't execute, it exhausts. It is based not on exclusion but on exurbanization. It expresses itself not as repression but as depression.

Infiltration, invasion, and infection are the modus operandi of macro-physical violence. They all assume a clear, immunologically effective separation of the self and the foreign. As a result of a lack of negativity, micro-physical violence displays an entirely different topology and pathological form. Infarction takes the place of infection. Macro-physical violence manifests expressively, explosively, explicitly, impulsively, and invasively. Micro-physical violence manifests implicitly and implosively.

Macro-physical violence de-internalizes the subject by penetrating its interior and annihilating it. The exterior destroys the interior. Micro-physical violence, in contrast,

de-internalizes the subject by *dissipating* it with excess positivity. Psychic illnesses such as ADD and ADHD are the consequences of this destructive *dissipation*. Destruction and
dissipation are not identical. Dissipation lacks the negativity
of the *other*. It results from too much of the *same*. Things
that have a dissipating effect are worldly, immanent events
that impose on perception. In contrast to macro-physical
violence, which is disjunctive and exclusive, micro-physical
violence is additive and inclusive. Macro-physical violence
also destroys any possibility of practice or activity. Its victims are cast into radical passivity. The destructive nature of
micro-physical violence, on the other hand, arises from an
excess of activity, which expresses itself as hyperactivity.
The macro-logic of violence follows the immunological
model. Violence comes from the immunological *other*,
which penetrates the self and negates it. Thus the self per-
ishes by the negativity of the other, provided it does not
manage to negate it. Immunological defense takes the form
of the negation of negation. The self asserts *itself* when
confronted with the other by negating its negativity. As an
immunological principle, the negation of negation generates freedom. But contemporary society is not immunologically structured. The other doesn't generate such a great
deal of negative tension. It lacks the existential momentum
that triggers an intensive immunological reaction. The
enemy, who according to Schmitt would simply be the
other, has positivized itself into the competitor today. Every
immune reaction is a reaction to otherness. Sartre's *L'enfer,
c'est les autres* is only thinkable in an immunological era.

Today, otherness is increasingly giving way to consumable difference, which does not provoke an immune reaction. It lacks the barbs of foreignness, which would elicit an intensive immune defense. The foreign has also positivized itself to the exotic other, which, unlike the immunological other, does not cause an immune reaction. Unlike the macro-logic of violence, its micro-logic is not based on the immunological model. The micro-logic of violence is the *logic of the same*.

The general promiscuity of contemporary society and the lack of an immunological other are mutually dependent. *Promiscuus* means mixed. Promiscuity requires a lack of immune reaction to the other. The hybridity that generally characterizes attitudes toward life today is diametrically opposed to immunity. Immunological hyperesthesia does not permit hybridity. Globalization forces the immunological threshold to be lowered because a strong immunological reaction to the other blocks globalization, which is a process, or rather an *excess*, of disinhibition and the dissolution of boundaries. The violence of positivity develops in the negativity-less space of the same. The lack of negativity leads to a *proliferation of the positive*, which does not meet with immunological resistance because of its immanence. It is a *terror of the same*.

II

THE MICRO-PHYSICS OF VIOLENCE

6. SYSTEMATIC VIOLENCE

The *situation* in which an act of violence occurs often arises from the *system* and the systematic *structure* in which it is embedded. Thus, manifest, expressive forms of violence can be traced back to these implicit structures, which establish and stabilize a system of domination but which withdraw from visibility. Johan Galtung's theory of "structural violence" is also based on the assumption of the structural mediation of violence. Structures built into the social system ensure that conditions of injustice are perpetuated. They codify unequal relations of power and the unequal opportunities that result from them without revealing their true nature.[1] Because of their invisibility, the victims of the ruling system's violence may not be directly aware of it. That is what makes it so efficient.

Galtung bases his thought on a very broad conception of violence: "... violence is present when human beings are being influenced so that their actual somatic and mental realizations are below their potential realizations."[2] The negativity of deprivation is fundamental to structural violence, preventing a fair distribution of resources and opportunities. This conception of violence is too general. It doesn't capture the aspect that actually defines violence and distinguishes it from other negative social influences. The fact that working-class children have worse educational opportunities than upper-class children isn't violence but rather injustice. If violence is used as shorthand for general social negativity, the contours of the idea become hazy.

Galtung's concept of violence fails to grasp the difference between power and violence. Thus he attributes violence to the hierarchies and orders that are the basis of power and ruling relationships. The oppressed are "deprived because the structure deprives them of chances to organize and bring their power to bear against the top dogs. ..."[3] The social structures don't give resistance any chance to develop. One must correctly conclude that it is possible to rule without exercising violence. Structural violence is not violence in the strict sense of the word. Rather, it is a rulership technique. It makes it possible to rule discreetly and much more efficiently than ruling by violence.

Bourdieu's "symbolic violence" also dwells within the social system itself. It inscribes itself in the habitual patterns of perception and behavior, which are accepted and repeated unquestioned. One affirms and perpetuates power relations when one habitually does what is respectable. *Banality* is the affirmation of the established power relations. Symbolic violence ensures that the order of rule is maintained without requiring the *expenditure of physical violence.* In this case, the affirmation of the ruling order is not conscious but rather reflexive and prereflective. Symbolic violence collapses comprehension of what *is* into compliance with *rule.* It stabilizes power relations very effectively because it makes them seem *natural*, like a fact that is questioned by no one, something that is-the-way-it-is.

Bourdieu also fails to differentiate clearly between power and violence. He uses power and violence almost synonymously: "All power has a symbolic dimension: it must receive a form of assent from those ruled, which is not based on the voluntary decision of an enlightened consciousness, but rather on the unmediated and prereflective subjugation of the socialized body."[4] Despite the proximity of power and violence, there is a structural difference between them. The symbolic dimension of power is what ensures that rule can be exercised *without violence.* The more prereflective assent the rulership generates symbolically, the less need it has for flagrant violence. If, on the other hand, it lacks symbolic mediation to habitualize it and make it automatic, it must be laboriously maintained with extensive tactics of violence and coercion.

Both structural and symbolic violence require a structure of rule, the hierarchical antagonistic relationship between classes. It is exercised by the ruling class on the ruled class, by those in power on those subject to it, by the "top dogs" on the "underdogs." Perpetrator and victim are distinct in this context. *Exploitation of the other* is the procedure. It turns symbolic-structural violence into a violence of negativity. Its victims are exposed to an *external* compulsion. It may be internalized, but it remains *foreign* to its host.

What Žižek calls "objective violence" hardly differs from symbolic-structural violence. Žižek himself speaks of "social-symbolic violence," which transforms ideology into a *natural* given fact that is confirmed by every conscious decision: "The same holds for violence. Social-symbolic violence at its purest appears as its opposite, as the spontaneity of the milieu in which we dwell, of the air we breathe."[5]

It generates "the more subtle forms of coercion that sustain relations of domination and exploitation."[6] It is violence immanent in the system, upstream of flagrant acts of violence, and yet invisible as such. Thus it is a violence of negativity that the ruling class exercises on those ruled. It dwells within "the social conditions of global capitalism," and produces "excluded and dispensable individuals from the homeless to the unemployed."[7] According to Žižek's argument, Agamben's *homines sacri* would represent the victim of this violence immanent in the system. In reference to the outbreak of violence in New Orleans, he writes: "The U.S., the world's policeman who endeavours to control threats to peace, freedom, and democracy around the globe, lost control of a part of America itself. For a few days, New Orleans apparently regressed to a wild preserve of looting, killing, and rape. It became a city of the dead and dying, a postapocalyptic zone where those the philosopher Giorgio Agamben calls *homines sacri*—people excluded from civil order—wander."[8]

In his theory of violence, Žižek adheres to the negativity model. In his conception, it erects a wall of exclusion and segregation: "The fundamental divide is one between those included in the sphere of (relative) economic prosperity and those excluded from it."[9] The victims of this violence aren't just *homines sacri* who live beyond the zone of well-being, eking out a bare existence, but also certain societal groups such as minorities or the unemployed. According to Žižek, Western society places "tremendous pressure" on "women in our liberal society," compelling them "to undergo such procedures as plastic surgery, cosmetic implants, and Botox injections in order to remain competitive in the sex market."[10] In this light, Western society, in which women *voluntarily* undergo the torture of cosmetic operations, does not differ fundamentally from African societies that subject women to painful genital mutilation.

In Žižek's argument, "objective violence" upholds the relations of rule and exploitation. In this case, exploitation is exploitation of the other. Žižek misses the *systematic violence* that takes place *without domination* and that leads to *self-exploitation*, affecting not merely a part but all of a society. The Western achievement society subjects not just women or the working class but *all* of its members to compulsion. Contrary to Žižek's assumption, men as well as women undergo cosmetic operations today in order to remain competitive on the market. The compulsion to optimize the body encompasses *everyone*, indiscriminately. It doesn't just produce Botox, silicone, and beauty zombies but also muscle, anabolic steroid, and fitness zombies. As a doping society, the society of achievement knows no class or gender differences. "Top dogs" are affected by the demand for performance and optimization just as "underdogs" are. *All* members of society are affected by burnout. Today it seems that we have *all* become performance and health zombies. The victims of this systemic violence aren't the excluded *homines sacri* but the achievement-subjects *trapped within* the system, who, as sovereigns and entrepreneurs of themselves, aren't subjugated to anyone. In a sense, they are free, but simultaneously, they are the *homo sacer of themselves.* Systemic violence is not the violence of exclusion. Instead it turns everyone into *captives*, prisoners of the system that forces them to exploit themselves.

Both Bourdieu's "symbolic violence" and Galtung's "structural violence" differ from this *systematic violence*, which affects *all* members of a social system indiscriminately, making them victims and therefore requiring no *antagonism* between the classes, no hierarchical relationship between those above and those below for its development. It occurs without enmity or domination. The subject who wields it is neither a power-holding person nor the ruling class but rather the *system itself.* Thus it lacks an *acting subject* who could be made responsible for its oppression and exploitation.

As *violence of positivity, systemic violence* completely lacks the negativity of restraint, rejection, prohibition, exclusion, or deprivation. It manifests as immoderation and amassment, as excess, exurbanization, and exhaustion, as overproduction, overaccumulation, overcommunication, and excess information. Because of its positivity, it is not perceived as violence. It is not only *too little* that leads to violence but also *too much*, not just the *negativity of prohibition* but also the *positivity of the ability to do everything.*

Today people increasingly react to this surplus of the same and excess of positivity with a psychic abreaction. *Psychic bulimia* ensues. It is not an *immunological* answer to negativity because excess of the same does not trigger the immune system. Thus the violence of positivity is

PART II

possibly more calamitous than the violence of negativity. Increasing neuronal disruptions such as depression or burnout are a telling symptom of the rejection and negation of the *prevailing rule*. The difference between the exploiter and the exploited disappears. "Top dogs" suffer from burnout just as "underdogs" do. The system's victims are also its accomplices. They cannot be distinguished from the perpetrators who ensure that the system functions smoothly. Violence becomes self-referential in that one exploits oneself, becoming perpetrator and victim at once.

7. THE MICRO-PHYSICS OF POWER

The thesis of Foucault's theory of power is the following: since the seventeenth century, power has no longer manifested as the deadly power of the sovereign but rather as disciplinary power and biopower. As the power of the sword, the sovereign's power threatens death. It culminates "in the privilege to seize hold of life in order to suppress it."[11] Disciplinary power, in contrast, works to "incite, reinforce, control, monitor, optimize, and organize the forces under it. ..." It focuses on "generating forces, making them grow, and ordering them, rather ... impeding them, making them submit, or destroying them."[12] It is not the deathly power of the sovereign but rather a life force "whose highest function was perhaps no longer to kill, but to invest life through and through."[13] The old power of death manifested in sovereignty "was now carefully supplanted by the administration of bodies and the calculated management of life."[14] Instead of martyring the body, disciplinary power confines it within a system of commands and prohibitions.

The power of sovereignty lacks the subtle maneuverings of disciplinary power, which penetrate into the narrowest corners of the body and psyche, where they achieve their effects. Foucault's "micro-physics of power" describes the procedures of power that produce norms and habits rather than pain and death, and that must "qualify, measure, appraise, and hierarchize, rather than display itself in its murderous splendor. ..."[15] In order to organize its subjects, "it [power] effects distributions around the norm." It is a power of normalization that conceals its identity as power and presents itself as society. He describes "normalizing society" as "the historical outcome of a technology of power centered on life." This technology of power discovered the "population" and made its appearance as "biopower": "propagation, births and mortality, the level of health, life expectancy and longevity, with all the conditions that can cause these to vary. Their supervision was effected through an entire series of interventions and *regulatory controls: a biopolitics of the population.*"[16]

The subject who wields deadly power is clearly defined: the godlike sovereign. But *who* is the *subject* who yields disciplinary power and biopower? Who is the ruler? Is life power or biopower actually *power in the true sense?* The progress of industrialization certainly made it necessary to discipline the body as well as the psyche, making them conform to the requirements of mechanized and industrial production. But this disciplinary method, which encompassed all areas of life, is not synonymous with methods of power and rule. In reality, Foucault isn't describing a new *form of power* but rather *a new form of society*: disciplinary society. As such, however, it does not represent a form of power and rule. Thus the power of sovereignty and disciplinary methods do not allow a direct comparison based on the economy of power. The disciplinary method is not a direct expression of power and rule but rather a general social practice. That is why the compulsions of disciplinary society affect not only the subjugated but all members and all classes of society, the ruler as well as the subject. Biopolitics is also not power politics as such. Neither the "adjustment of the accumulation of men to that of capital" nor "the joining of the growth of human groups to the expansion of productive forces"[17] is a genuine practice of power and rule.

In the modern era, a diffusion and scattering of power has taken place; indeed, it is an increasing *disempowerment of power*.[18] It apparently misleads Foucault to define power itself as "nonsubjective," that is, as a purely structural "multiplicity of force relations immanent in the sphere in which they operate and which constitute their own organization. ..."[19] He attempts to conceive of power without "a general system of domination exerted by one group over another, a system whose effects, through successive derivations, pervade the entire social body."[20] But it is utterly impossible to think of power outside any relation of domination or hierarchical social order. Furthermore, power necessarily requires *subjectivity*, a subjective intentionality. In that sense it differs from force or relations of force.

Foucault apparently envisions a desubjectified relation of power: "Power relations are both intentional and nonsubjective."[21] Nonsubjective intentionality is an oxymoron. Only later did Foucault recognize the weaknesses of his purely structural conception of power, reintroducing subjectivity into relations of power: "Power exists only when it is put into action, even if, of course, it is integrated into a disparate field of possibilities brought to bear upon permanent structures."[22] Power establishes solid structures in order to stabilize itself, or to establish its position in a disparate field of possibilities. But it doesn't thrive on them. They are simply its medium.

Foucault points to the fact that war was never bloodier than in the nineteenth century. Monstrous deadly violence could expand across borders with such elan and cynicism precisely because it "exerts a positive influence on life, which endeavors to administer, optimize, and multiply it, subjecting it to precise controls and comprehensive regulations."[23] Wars were no longer waged in the name of the sovereign who had to be defended but rather "on behalf of the existence of everyone," the entire "population" or the "habitants": "It is as managers of life and survival, of bodies and the race, that so many regimes have been able to wage so many wars, causing so many men to be killed. ... The principle underlying the tactics of battle—that one has to be capable of killing in order to go on living—has become the principle that defines the strategy of states. But the existence in question is no longer the juridical existence of sovereignty; at stake is the biological existence of a population."[24]

Wars waged in the name of a "nation" or a "people" or even "on behalf of the existence of everyone" unleash more deadly violence than all the wars waged in the name of a sovereign. But this deadly violence directed toward *other* nations is not inherent in that "positive influence on life" whose telos is "to invest life through and through."

Foucault apparently lacks the sensory faculties to detect violence. Thus, he thinks of torture in terms of the production of truth,[25] without considering its internal economy of violence and pleasure. He also misses the violence at the heart of suicide. He points out that suicide, which, "once a crime, since it was a way to usurp the power of death which the sovereign alone ... had the right to exercise" in "a society in which political power had assigned itself the task of administering life," shifted into the scope of sociological analysis. He takes suicide to be a natural event, one "so persistent and constant" that it deserves no particular attention.[26] And so he does not concern himself with the rapid increase in this violence against the self in the so-called disciplinary society. It points to the immanent structures of violence within the society, which remain hidden to Foucault.

In the introduction to *Homo Sacer*, Agamben speaks of the "curious fact" that "Foucault ... never dwelt on the exemplary places of modern biopolitics: the concentration camp and the structure of the great totalitarian states of the twentieth century."[27] Agamben blames Foucault's untimely death for this "curious fact." He believes that Foucault did not have time to explore all the implications of the concept of biopolitics and to indicate the direction in which he would have pursued his research. Agamben does not take note of the fact that Foucault's theory of biopolitics is laid out in such a way that it *cannot* include the deadly violence of the camps. The *difference between prison and camp* eludes it. The prison is a constitutive element in a locality within disciplinary society. The camp is a *non-place*. Foucaultian biopolitics, which focuses on the "administration of bodies and the calculated management of life," cannot access the camp as a non-place. The deadly violence of the camp stands in opposition to the biopolitical economy, which aims "to invest life through and through." Foucault's *Discipline and Punish* closes with the following words: "In this central and centralized humanity, the effect and instrument of complex power relations, bodies and forces subjected by multiple mechanisms of 'incarceration,' objects for discourses that are in themselves elements for this strategy, we must hear the distant roar of battle."[28] Foucault's disciplinary society of prisons, hospitals, jails, barracks, and factories no longer reflects contemporary society. A society of glass office towers, shopping malls, fitness centers, yoga studios, and beauty clinics long ago took its place. Twenty-first-century society is not a disciplinary society but rather a society of achievement. The high walls of the disciplinary society now seem archaic. They belong to a society of negativity, which was governed by commands and prohibitions.

The obedience-subject is subordinated to a ruling authority, which exploits it. "Deduction," which is inherent in the power of sovereignty, according to Foucault, is exploitation of the other. Unlike the obedience-subject, the achievement-subject is free because it is dominated by no one. Its psychic constitution is not determined by *should* but by *can*. It must be its own master. Its existence is not governed by commands and prohibitions but rather by freedom and initiative. The imperative for performance transforms freedom into compulsion. Self-exploitation replaces exploitation of the other. The achievement-subject exploits itself until it collapses completely. Here, violence and freedom coincide, making violence self-targeting. The exploiter is the exploited. The perpetrator is also the victim. Burnout is the pathological emanation of this paradoxical freedom.

Thus the violence of positivity is more insidious than the violence of negativity because it masquerades as freedom. The "distant roar of battle" has not been silenced. However, it arises from an unusual battle, one without domination or enmity. One wages war against oneself and does violence to oneself. It no longer sounds from the disciplinary society's institutions of incarceration but rather from the *psyche of the achievement-subject.* Paradoxically, this new prison is called freedom. It's like a labor camp where one is prisoner and warden at once.

The violence of *decapitation* belonged to the premodern society of sovereignty. Its medium is blood. Modern disciplinary society continued to be a society of negativity. It was governed by disciplinary compulsion, "social orthopedics." *Deformation* is its form of violence. But neither *decapitation* nor *deformation* describes the late modern achievement society. It is ruled by the violence of positivity, which makes freedom indistinguishable from compulsion. Its pathological symptom is *depression*.

8.   THE VIOLENCE OF POSITIVITY

Religion is a *system of negativity*. With its commands, prohibitions, and rituals, it prevents the proliferation of positivity. It gives rise to clear contours and spaces with high semantic and atmospheric tension. In so doing, it holds the *entropy* of the social system at a very low level. In contrast, the orgy of liberation, deregulation, dissolution of boundaries, and deritualization that continues to this day extensively reduces negativity. The reduction of negativity generates a glut of positivity, a general promiscuity, an excess of mobility, of consumption, of communication, of information, and of production.

The accumulation of the positive blocks and congests the circulation, causing the system to collapse. After a certain point, information is no longer informative, production is no longer productive, and communication is no longer communicative. Everything grows and proliferates beyond its goal, beyond its purpose, indeed, beyond the economy of use. Baudrillard writes: "The uninterrupted production of positivity has a terrifying consequence. Whereas negativity engenders crisis and critique, hyperbolic positivity for its part engenders catastrophe. ... Any structure that hunts down, expels or exorcizes its negative elements risks catastrophe caused by a thoroughgoing backlash, just as any organism that hunts down and eliminates its germs, bacteria, parasites or other biological antagonists risks metastasis and cancer—in other words, it is threatened by a voracious positivity of its own cells, or, in the viral context, by the prospect of being devoured by its own—now unemployed—antibodies. Anything that purges the accursed share in itself signs its own death warrant. This is the theorem of the accursed share."[29] Problematically, Baudrillard is following the conventional formula of repression and return. The exclusion of the other or the accursed share evokes a different sort of otherness. It is assumed that the aseptic space of positivity, from which the other's immunologically effective negativity has been eliminated, develops new forms of virality and pathology: "He who lives by the same shall die by the same. The absence of otherness secretes another, intangible otherness: the absolute other of the virus. The spectre of the Same had struck again. In every compulsion to resemblance, every extradition of difference ... lies the threat of an incestuous virulence, a diabolical otherness. ... This is the reappearance of the principle of Evil in a new guise."[30] Modern medicine, Baudrillard continues, fails to understand this new pathology of incestuous virulence when it treats cancer and AIDS as if they were conventional illnesses, although they actually arise from the triumph of prophylaxis. They are illnesses that result from the disappearance of illness, from the eradication of pathogenic forms, and that thus do not respond to the treatments of earlier eras. "[A] third-level pathology," is at play, "one that is inaccessible to the pharmacopoeia of an earlier period. ..."[31]

By this point, Baudrillard's theory of virulence has lost its argumentative stringency, since HIV does not differ fundamentally from other viruses. Like every virus, it displays the negativity of the immunological other. In principle, it is possible to fight the virus with antibodies. Healing is the immunological negation of negation. Nor is autoimmunity what makes cancer so deadly, though Baudrillard presumes that it causes the organism to be destroyed by its own otherwise unoccupied antibodies. A cancerous cell is one that has mutated to become *other*, and that therefore remains the object of immune defense. Computer viruses also assume negativity, which is countered by antivirus programs. Viral violence, which is also exercised by HIV, cancer, and computer viruses, is a violence of negativity. But our era is not a viral one. Its exemplary illnesses are not viral or bacterial infections but rather psychic ailments such as burnout, hyperactivity, and depression, which are caused not by viral negativity but rather by excess positivity and the violence of positivity.

Baudrillard doesn't grasp the pathology of the positive because he continues to adhere to the immunological model: "All the talk of immunity, antibodies, grafting and rejection should not surprise anyone. In periods of scarcity, absorption and assimilation are the order of the day. In periods of abundance, rejection and expulsion are the chief concerns. Today, generalized communication and surplus information threaten to overwhelm all human defenses."[32] The excess of overproduction, overachievement, overconsumption, overcommunication, and over-information threatens not only the immune system but also the psychic-neuronal system. The pathology of the positive has nothing to do with the immune system. There is no immune reaction to the obesity of the system. Fat can be *burned*, not *repelled*. Owing to its positivity, the *same* does not result in the production of antibodies. It does not make sense to strengthen defenses to combat the violence of the *same*. They only defend against the other. There is also a difference between immunological and nonimmunological repulsion. *Disgust* is a sort of immune reaction because it is directed at the *other*. Too much of the *same* might cause vomiting, but that isn't an immunological defense but rather a digestive-psychic *abreaction*.

In an interview with *Der Spiegel,* Baudrillard pointed to the altered form of the battle: "There is no front anymore and no line of demarcation. The enemy is in the heart of the culture battling against it. It is the Fourth World War, if you will: it is no longer between people, nations, systems, or ideologies. ..."[33] Baudrillard doesn't recognize that the new world war takes place *without an enemy* who could be "battled." Rather, one is *at war with oneself.* Owing to the lack of negativity, enmity becomes *self-referential.* Those who destroy are destroyed. Those who strike are struck. Those who triumph lose simultaneously. Since it purports to be peace, this war is neither visible nor public. It is a war that no one can win. This war without enmity wouldn't be ended by the victory of one party over the other but only by global collapse, *global burnout.* The entire system would overheat until it imploded. *Implosive* violence is at work here. It differs from *explosive* violence, which expands and conquers new territories as imperial violence or as the violence of classic warfare. Explosive violence creates pressure outward. Because of the lack of an exterior, implosive violence pushes inward. Inside, it generates destructive tensions and compulsions that cause the *collapse* of the entire system. Climate and environmental catastrophes also point to the overheating of the system. The achievement-subject's burnout is a pathological precursor to the imminent implosion of the system.

According to Baudrillard's genealogy of enmity, in the first stage the enemy is the wolf. It is "an external enemy who attacks and against whom one defends oneself by building fortifications and erecting walls."[34] In later stages of its genealogy, the enemy progressively loses its substance and visibility. It shrinks and conceals itself. In the second stage it appears as a rat, which operates underground, necessitating a new defense strategy. Walls and fences are useless against it. Only "hygiene" or techniques of cleanliness keep its danger at bay. After the third stage, the beetle, the enemy finally takes on viral form: "Viruses are the fourth stage. ... It is much more difficult to defend oneself against viruses because they exist in the heart of the system."[35] Now "a ghostly enemy emerged, infiltrating itself throughout the whole planet, slipping in everywhere like a virus, welling up from all the interstices of power."[36] According to Baudrillard, the panic following the anthrax attacks reflects morphological and topological changes in violence and enmity. Viral sleeper cells that inhabit the system operate against the system as enemies as soon as they are activated. They form an exterior in the interior. They attack the system as forces external to it. In this case, there is a clear difference between perpetrator and victim. Furthermore, "viral violence" is governed by antagonistic tension. It is a violence of negativity. As enemy, the terrorist is the immunological other in the system, which it infiltrates and destroys.

Baudrillard totalizes the viral violence of terrorism as *the* exemplary form of violence today. Islamic terrorism is just one of its variations. "[T]error against terror" is at hand, the terror of singularity against the terror of globalization, which for its part is based on "monstrous violence." Terrorism is "everywhere," "in each of us." It makes use of "any arbitrary actor, all of us as possible accomplices." It is "perceptible everywhere and visible in every form of violence, be it human, accidental, or catastrophic."[37] The "homogenizing, dissolving power" of the global brings with it "heterogeneous forces" that are "not merely different, but antagonistic."[38] Baudrillard promotes resistance to the violence of globalization by countering it with "radical singularity, the event of singularity." He heralds the "uprising of singularity."[39] Like Antonio Negri, Baudrillard lapses into a postmodern romanticism of singularity. Contrary to his thesis, social antagonism is not developing between the global and the singular today. Contemporary society, which displays increasing erosion of the social, produces scattered, self-focused selves with weak connections to a "we," existing under intensely competitive conditions. They are not singularities, which together could be in a position to resist the global. Rather, they are all simultaneously hangers-on, accomplices, and victims of the global. They are micro-entrepreneurs who can only have business relations, if any. Today, Islamic terrorism is no longer really a threat. Much more dangerous than the *terror of the other* is the *terror of the same, the terror of immanence.* No effective defense against the latter is possible owing to its lack of negativity.

Baudrillard erroneously characterizes the violence of the global as a viral violence. He writes: "It is a viral violence, that of the net and of the virtual. A violence of gentle annihilation, a genetic and communicative violence, a violence of consensus and forced interaction. ... This violence is viral: it operates by contagion, by chain reaction, and it gradually destroys all our immunities. ..."[40] The communication of the global is a postimmunological communication. The lack of immunological negativity results in overcommunication. The resulting mass of communication causes increasing entropy in the system. *Infection* is a new form of communication. It is not a *communication of meaning* because it occurs via affective intensity and impulses. Contrary to Baudrillard's assumption, it lacks the negativity of the viral.

The temporal crisis of today is not acceleration. Acceleration in itself is not inherently destructive. Accelerated cell growth can be temporarily useful, provided it works to benefit the economy of the entire organism. If acceleration overshoots any useful purpose and takes on a life of its own, it assumes a diabolic form. This sort of accelerated growth is no longer growth but rather an excrescence. True acceleration follows a process that is directed at a goal. What is regarded as acceleration today is actually a *rapid increase in entropy*, which causes things to run riot and proliferate, generating a saturated, suffocating mass.

Bacilli destroy their environment not perhaps because they intend to destroy it but because they degenerate into blind, excessive growth. They are blind to the higher entity to which they owe their life and survival. Schnitzler proposes a relationship between bacilli and the human race: "Were we to suppose that the human race represented an illness for some higher organism completely inconceivable to us, within which was to be found the purpose, necessity, and meaning of their existence, but which they also sought to destroy, and indeed would ultimately have to destroy, the more highly developed they became—just so do the race of bacilli strive to annihilate the 'ailing' human individual! Even were this supposition to approach the truth—our powers of imagination wouldn't know what to make of it; for our intellect is only capable of grasping what is downward and deeper, never what is upward and higher; only that which is *lower* can be relatively known to us, but we can only guess at the *higher*. Thus, perhaps we can conceive of the history of humanity as its eternal struggle against the divine, which, despite its best resistance, gradually but necessarily is annihilated by the human. ..."[41] In light of the destructive excess growth in many areas of life, Freud's death drive thesis gains plausibility. The forces that at first glance appeared to be progress and vitality, which represent the hyperactivity of the late modern achievement society, would then be destructive impulses arising from the death drive, ultimately leading to the deadly collapse of the entire system—that is, its *burnout*.

9. THE VIOLENCE OF TRANSPARENCY

The buzzword *transparency* dominates social discourse today. A comprehensive process is under way, a paradigm shift whose complexity and effects penetrate far beyond the problems of democracy, justice, and truth. The current compulsion for transparency points to a social configuration that is dominated by *excess positivity* and thereby progressively reduces *negativity*. The dismantling of thresholds, differences, and borders leads to various forms of proliferation and congestion of social circulatory systems. Thus the dictate for transparency cannot be separated from phenomena like *hypercommunication, hyperinformation,* and *hypervisibility*.

The *negativity* of the inaccessible determines the topology of the sacred. Sacred spaces are exclusive spaces, which are closed off and separated from the outside. Thresholds protect them from being profaned. The religious experience is a threshold experience, an experience of the *completely other*. As a society of positivity, the transparent society removes every threshold and every threshold experience by leveling everything to the same. The *transcendence of the completely other* yields to the *transparency of the same.* After all, thresholds block vision, which has been unleashed as hypervisibility today. They also rein in the general promiscuity and permeability that characterize the transparent society.

It is incommensurable otherness that prevents a system from entirely corresponding with itself, which is to say, from being transparent to itself. But self-transparency is not the telos of every system. For many systems the impossibility of their transparency is the condition for their possibility. In matters of faith, there is no question of transparency. This distinguishes them from the system of knowledge, whose telos is self-transparency. The negativity of not-knowing is also constitutive of trust. Where there is certainty, trust is superfluous because it is a condition between knowing and not knowing. Thinking and total transparency are also mutually exclusive. Thinking positivizes into *calculation.* Unlike calculation, thinking *gathers experience* by transforming and by *making other*: "To undergo an experience with something—be it a thing, a person, or a god—means that this something befalls us, strikes us, comes over us, overwhelms and transforms us."[42] The German word *Geist* (*psyche, spirit*) originally meant agitation or emotional turmoil, indicating that it is never completely transparent. Self-transparency does not radiate unrest or turmoil. The constant demand for transparency is based on an idea of the world and of human beings that is free of all negativity. Only a machine is transparent, however. Transparent communication would be machine communication, which humans wouldn't be capable of. The compulsion to total transparency reduces humans themselves to functional elements in a system. That is the violence of transparency. A person's integrity requires a certain inaccessibility and impermeability. Total illumination and overexposure of the person would be violence. Thus Peter Handke writes: "I live on what others don't know about me."[43]

Transparency is not produced by friendly light that allows the particular to appear in its particularity, the arbitrary in its lovely arbitrariness, that is, the other in its incommensurable otherness. Instead, the general politics of transparency makes otherness disappear by driving it into the *light of the same.* Transparency is achieved by eliminating what is other. The violence of transparency ultimately expresses itself as the reduction of the other to the same, as the elimination of otherness. It draws on re-*semblance.* The politics of transparency is a *dictatorship of the same.*

The imperative for transparency accelerates communication by eliminating all negativity, which would otherwise necessitate lingering, pausing, or hesitating. Communication reaches maximum speed *where the same answers the same*, where a *chain reaction of the same* takes place. Otherness, in contrast, delays it. Transparent language is a mechanized, functional language completely lacking ambivalence. The diktat of transparency annihilates the vague, the opaque, the complex. Counting is more transparent than recounting. Addition is more transparent than narration. Unlike stories, numbers have no fragrance. Transparency also robs time of scent. Transparent time is time without scent, time without events, time without narration, time without scenes. If the narrative thread disappears completely from time, it disintegrates into a mere succession, a scattered, atomized present. Nor is memory *transparent to itself* because unlike storage space, which simply works narratively, memory displays narrative structure. Because of their historicity and narrativity, traces of memory are constantly subject to reordering and rewriting.[44] Data that are saved always remain the *same*.

Politics as such is *strategic action*. Spheres of secrecy are integral to it. They distinguish it from mere administration and management, which would just be *work*. Political action is not *work*. Disclosing all intention also makes *playing a game* impossible, because that too is strategic action. Where strategy is impossible, there can only be statistics such as polls. According to Carl Schmitt, "The postulate of openness finds its specific opponent in the idea that the Arcana belong to every kind of politics, political-technical secrets that in fact are just as necessary for absolutism as business and economic secrets are for an economic life that depends on private property and competition."[45] Without a sphere of secrecy, politics degenerates into theatrocracy, which can't do without a stage and spectators. "The eighteenth century staked much on self-confidence and the aristocratic concept of secrecy. In a society that no longer has such courage, there can be no more 'arcana,' no more hierarchy, no more secret diplomacy; in fact, no more politics. To every great politics belongs the 'arcanum.' Everything will take place on stage (before an audience of papagenos)."[46] Schmitt's politics of violence is a politics of secrecy. The more political an action is, the more secrecy it generates. Thus Schmitt calls on politics to have more "courage to secrecy."[47] Power or rulership and transparency are not compatible. Schmitt's idea of sovereignty requires absolute negativity. The sovereign decides on the state of exception. The state of exception, in which the entire legal order is in question, is a *state of absolute nontransparency.*

The imperative for transparency makes all distance and discretion disappear. Transparency means total proximity and lack of distance, total promiscuity and permeability, total exposure and exhibition. Transparency is also the nakedness and obscenity of money, which makes everything equivalent to everything else by abolishing the incommensurability and impenetrability of things. A world in which everything can be expressed in terms of price and in which everything must produce a profit is obscene. Furthermore, the society of transparency is one in which everything is *on display.* In this *exposed society,* every subject is its own product for sale. Everything is measured by its *exhibition value. Cult value,* which consists not in being-exposed but in being-there (*Da-Sein*), disappears completely. Exposed society is pornographic society. Everything is oriented outward, stripped, bare, unveiled, and denuded. The exposed countenance without any "aura of looking"[48] flattens into a mere *face.* The *face* is the commercialized form of the countenance. Excessive exhibition turns everything into a product that is "doomed, naked and with no secret, to immediate devouring." Total exhibition is obscene in its totally uninhibited putting-on-display. Hypervisibility is obscene. Things don't disappear in the dark but rather in the overexposure of hypervisibility: "More generally, visible things do not terminate in obscurity and in silence; they vanish into what is more visible than the visible: obscenity."[49]

The total elimination of borders and thresholds is pornographic. The smooth, unbroken streams of hyperinformation and hypercommunication are also obscene, lacking the negativity of the secret, the inaccessible, or the hidden. The compulsion to render everything communicable and visible is also obscene. Communication without scenography is pornography. At the sexual level, obscenity is "the loss of the scenic illusion of desire to an exhibition, a direct promiscuity of bodies."[50]

Contemporary transparency society is characterized by pornographic exhibition that converges with panoptic control. As an electronic panopticon, the net feeds on exhibition and voyeurism. Control society reaches its apogee when its subjects expose themselves not under outside coercion but through a *self-generated need*, that is, when fear of losing the private and intimate sphere yields to the need to place those spheres shamelessly on display. The society of achievement also reaches maximum efficiency when freedom and self-exploitation are indistinguishable. *Self-exposure* and *self-exploitation* merge.

The compulsion for transparency is ultimately not an ethical or political imperative but rather an economic one. *Exposure is exploitation. Communication is commerce.* Someone who is completely exposed is completely vulnerable to exploitation. Overilluminating a person maximizes their economic efficiency. The *transparent customer* is the new inhabitant, indeed, the *homo sacer* of the economic panopticon. The panopticon of the consumption and achievement society differs from the panopticon of the disciplinary society in that it requires no shackles, no walls, no closed spaces. Now the *whole* society, the *entire* globe, is a panopticon. Google and social networks like Facebook are also *digital panopticons* for secret services. Search terms and profiles surrender a person to panoptic observation and control. Analyzing the data that individuals feed into the net would make them more transparent than they could ever be to themselves. The net forgets nothing and represses nothing. Unlike the panopticon of the disciplinary society, panoptic control does not occur by means of isolation and confinement but rather by interconnection. Today, surveillance does not take the form of an *attack on freedom.* Rather, freedom and control are one. One surrenders oneself *voluntarily* to the panoptic gaze. The transparent user is victim and perpetrator at once. Everyone is at work diligently building the panopticon of the net. Free communication and panoptic control fuse and become indistinguishable.

10. THE MEDIUM IS THE MASS-AGE

Language is a medium of communication. Like every medium, it expresses itself symbolically as well as diabolically. Thus it is helpful to presume that language has two different functional variations: the symbolic and the diabolic. Raising consensus to *the* essence of language misses the diabolic function of language.[51] Aligning language so closely with violence, on the other hand, misses its symbolic, communicative dimension.[52] *Symballein* means to connect. Because of its symbolic function, language is connective, that is, communicative. But a *symbolon* implies a *diabolon*. *Diaballein* means to separate and divide. Because of its diabolic function, language isn't connective only but also divisive and injurious. The symbolic side of language is constructive and communicative. The diabolic side lends it its destructive characteristics.

The positivizing of society also affects language, producing an entirely different form of linguistic violence. This violent language relies on defamation, discrediting, degradation, disavowal, and reification, and is a violence of negativity.[53] In this case *the other* is negated. It follows the *immunological formula* of friend and enemy. The new violence of language isn't negative but positive. It is not directed *against the other*. Rather, it arises from a mass of the *same*, an accumulation of the positive.

In contemporary society, overcommunication causes *spamification of language and communication*. It accumulates masses of communication and information that are neither informative nor communicative. This term doesn't refer just to spam in the narrow sense, which increasingly litters communication, but also to the masses of communication produced by practices like microblogging.[54] The Latin word *communicare* means to do something together, to unite, to give, or to have something in common.

Communication is a community-building act. But after a certain point it is no longer communicative, only *cumulative*. Information is informative because it expresses ideas *in a form*. After a certain point, information is no longer in-formative but rather de-formative. It is *out of form*.

The spamification of language is accompanied by *hypertrophy of the ego*, which generates *communicative emptiness*. It has ushered in a *post-Cartesian shift*. The Cartesian self is a fragile entity. It is preceded by radical doubt. It was born as a hesitant assumption. "In rejecting—and even imagining to be false—everything which we can in any way doubt, it is easy for us to suppose that there is no God and no heaven, and that there are no bodies, and even that we ourselves have no hands or feet, or indeed any body at all. But we cannot for all that suppose that we, who are having such thoughts, are nothing. For it is a contradiction to suppose that what thinks does not, at the very time when it is thinking, exist. ... *I am thinking, therefore I exist*. ..."[55] The post-Cartesian self is no longer a tentative assumption but a solid reality. It is not a cautious formulation but a primordial determination. The post-Cartesian self doesn't even have to negate the other in order to position itself. In this sense, it differs from the Cartesian appropriation-subject, which posits itself, defines itself, and positions itself by means of negating the other, and which designates its borders, defines its identity, and marks its territory by delimiting itself from the other. Carl Schmitt's formulation does not apply to the post-Cartesian, postimmunological self: "The enemy is our own question as *Gestalt*." According to Schmitt, the self owes its identity, its *"Gestalt,"* to the other as the enemy, who must be negated. The post-Cartesian self lacks this negativity of immunological delimitation and defense.

A total inversion of the Cartesian formulation takes place as a result of the positivity of the post-Cartesian self. In his book *Consuming Life,* Zygmunt Bauman draws on the old Cartesian formula: "I shop, therefore I am."[56] The post-Cartesian inversion of the formula apparently escapes Baumann. The Cartesian formula *I shop, therefore I am* no longer rings true. It really should be: I am, therefore I shop. *I am, therefore I dream, I feel, I love, I doubt, I even think; sum ergo cogito.* Sum, ergo dubito. Sum, ergo credo, and so on. The redundancy and recursion of the post-Cartesian I-am is apparent. Practices like microblogging are also dominated by hypertrophied selves. Tweets can ultimately be reduced to *I-am.* It is a postimmunological self. In the boundless space of the net, it courts the attention of the other instead of warding it off or isolating itself from it.

For Heidegger, the language of the post-Cartesian self would be a *posthermeneutical* language without a "message." Heidegger's "message-bearing" (*Botengang*) or "message bearer" (*Botengänger*) juts into the hidden kerygmatic space from which the redundancy and evidence of the I-am withdraws. The language of the post-Cartesian I-am, on the other hand, is stripped of any hiddenness or secrecy. In its bareness and secretless exposure, it speaks a *posthermeneutical* language. According to Heidegger, "hermeneutic" means to stand in relation to that which the self-referential I-am overcomes.[57]

It is often claimed, invoking Lévinas, that it is already violence that *I* speak.[58] When *I* take the floor, I take it from someone else. From this perspective, the *I* itself is violence. Lévinas confronts this I with infinite responsibility, extending beyond "what I may or may not have done to the Other or whatever acts I may or may not have committed, as if I were devoted to the other man before being devoted to myself."[59] It exposes me to the other. Without this radical exposure to the other, says Lévinas, the self "thickens into a substance." The "violence" that turns me into the accused originates with the other.[60] Without this violent inflection, the self would return to its original position, which is violence. Lévinas's ethics is ultimately an *ethics of violence.*

The post-Cartesian self is neither "exposed" to the "other" nor trapped in the relations of domination. However, it isn't free from compulsion. It voluntarily subjects itself to the *compulsion to exhibition.* In Lévinas, exposure to the other increases "responsibility" to the point of "stripping beyond nudity" and "denuding itself of its skin."[61] These lines address the *ethical* subject in the emphatic sense. The post-Cartesian self, in contrast, appears as an *aesthetic* subject, which exhibits itself to the point of complete exposure, indeed, of pornographic nakedness. It must *exploit its exhibition value.* For the exposed, exhibited self, the other is a *spectator* and consumer. Lévinas's self still defines itself through the negation of the other. It takes up space by shutting the other out. The post-Cartesian self doesn't even require the negation of the other in order to position itself.

Overcommunication increases the *entropy* of the communication system. It creates waste-communication and language. In *Malfeasance: Appropriation through Pollution?* Michel Serres traces the origins of pollution and contamination back to the animalistic rabidity for appropriation. Animals claim their territory by marking it with foul-smelling urine and feces. One spits in the soup to deter fellow tablemates. Nightingales claim territory by driving others out with their noise. Serres distinguishes between two different kinds of garbage. Hard pollution consists of material waste, such as the contents of giant landfills, environmental toxins, or industrial waste. Soft pollution consists of linguistic, symbolic, and communicative garbage. The desire for acquisition suffocates the planet with garbage in a tsunami of symbols, leaving "a planet completely covered with garbage and billboards, lakes saturated with waste, submarine ditches overflowing with plastics, seas covered with debris. ... On each mountain rock, each tree leaf, each agricultural plot of land, you have advertisements; letters are written on each blade of grass. ... Like the legendary cathedrals, the landscape is swallowed by the tsunami of signs."[62]

Serres's creatures are still Cartesian in the sense that they follow the immunological principal in their territorial appropriation. They repel others as enemies with their foul-smelling urine and feces or their noise. Thus Serres writes: "Poor Descartes ratified our animal customs."[63] The pollution and contamination of the world today extend far beyond the scope of "Cartesian" appropriation. This is also key to the post-Cartesian revolution. Post-Cartesian garbage doesn't stink the way Cartesian excrement does. It even cloaks itself in the *beautiful*, in beautiful advertisement intended to draw attention. Serres's stinking garbage only accrues in the case of animalistic appropriation: "[A]s we shall see and hear, signs will quickly become just as dirty and polluting as the discharges and will perpetuate the ancient gestures of appropriation with their hard softness."[64]

The pollution and contamination of the world cannot be entirely attributed to *territorial* demarcation and appropriation. It takes place in a boundless, deterritorialized world. The point is not to conquer territory by driving others out of it but rather to get attention. Thus even garbage is *positivized* today. The *negative garbage* of appropriation repels others with its smell and noise. It creates territorial boundaries. *Positive garbage* is used to attract the attention of others. It must be pleasing to them. Negative garbage produces exclusion. Inclusion is the aim of positive garbage. It is not repellent. Rather, it must be appealing and attractive. Today's post-Cartesian nightingales don't twitter because they want to drive others out of their space. *They twitter for attention instead.*

Communication creates proximity. But more communication doesn't automatically produce greater proximity. At some point, excess proximity lapses into *distanceless indifference*. That is the *dialectic of proximity*. Excess proximity destroys proximity, which is *closer* than distancelessness. It is a proximity that is stimulated by distance. But in a glut of positive proximity, it disappears. The accumulation of the positive, of excess positivity, leads to deadening and dissipation, even to a callousing of perception that makes it blind to inconspicuous, hesitant, quiet, discreet, subtle things. Thus Michel Serres writes: "*Imperious images and letters force us to read, while the pleading things of the world are begging our senses for meaning. The latter ask; the former command.* Our senses give meaning to the world; our products already have meaning, which is flat. They are easier to perceive because they are less elaborate, similar to waste. Images are the waste of paintings; logos, the waste of writing; ads, the waste of vision; announcements, the residues of music. Forcing themselves on our perception, those low and facile signs clog up the landscape, which itself is more difficult, discreet, silent, and often dying because unseen by any saving perception."[65]

Serres attributes the world's pollution to the Cartesian subject's will to appropriate. But appropriation alone can't account for overcommunication and overproduction that defy economic rationality. Even bestial appropriation is determined by economic necessity. An animal secures itself the *necessary* habitat. Today's overproduction and overaccumulation, in contrast, are *transeconomic.* They transcend use value and break the economic tie between means and end. The end no longer provides a border or limit for the means. Overproduction and overaccumulation become self-referential and without proportion. Growth is diabolized into outgrowths and proliferation. Everything grows beyond its true purpose, which leads to clogging and congestion of the system: "So many things have been produced and accumulated that they can never possibly all be put to use. ... So many messages and signals are produced and disseminated that they can never possibly all be read."[66] In this light, overcommunication would be an uninterrupted fiction of the screen that competes with the void of the idiot box, a "forced scenario" that attempts to balance the *lack of being* with an excess of positivity.

This mass of communication, information, and signs emits a particular violence of positivity, one that no longer elucidates and informs because it is merely a *mass*. The positive *mass without message* scatters, dulls, and paralyzes. With just one small adjustment, McLuhan's "The medium is the message" can be tailored to the era of positive accumulation: *The medium is the mass-age.*

11.   RHIZOMATIC VIOLENCE

Violence originates not only with overcodification, which razes all free spaces with its rigid, repressive order, but also with unbounded decoding and dissolution of boundaries, which releases the world into a flood of undirected events, stimuli, and energies. Coding in itself is not violence. It articulates, structures, forms, orders, and verbalizes the world. Only totalitarian over- or hypercoding is violence. Undoubtedly, a certain decoding *can* free the world from its compulsions and constraints by working against repressive overcoding. But if it is intensified diabolically, it itself becomes destructive. Deleuze undialectically celebrates unbounded decoding as liberation, masking its diabolic side.

Cancerous proliferation, which overruns all organs, nullifying organic difference, is a diabolic form of decoding and deterritorialization. Deleuze's "body without organs," in which organic codification has been abolished, hardly differs from a body overrun with metastases. In it, all organic articulation is destroyed. *Essence* is abolished. De-essentialization intensifies into the diabolic. Deleuze's example of the organless body is the "schizophrenic table" that resembles a heap instead of a table and is divested of all functionality. The tabletop shrinks and then vanishes. It "disappears" in relation to the framework. Language itself is decoded and undifferentiated into an unarticulated mass of sounds: "In order to resist organ-machines, the body without organs presents its smooth, slippery, opaque, taut surface as a barrier. In order to resist linked, connected, and interrupted flows, it sets up a counterflow of amorphous, undifferentiated fluid. In order to resist using words composed of articulated phonetic units, it utters only gasps and cries that are sheer unarticulated blocks of sound."[67] Thus, Deleuze's "rhizome"[68] proliferates out of control: "A rhizome has no beginning or end; it is always in the middle, between things, interbeing, *intermezzo*. The tree is filiation, but the rhizome is alliance, uniquely alliance. The tree imposes the verb 'to be,' but the fabric of the rhizome is the conjunction, 'and ... and ... and. ...' This conjunction carries enough force to shake and uproot the verb 'to be.'"[69] Violence isn't merely the repressive *neither-nor* or the manipulative *either-or* but also the endless "and ... and ... and. ..." The accelerated *addition of the same* and excessive positivity cause a violent *abreaction*, which differs from immunological *defense* because of its positivity. *Psychic bulimia* doesn't follow the principles of immunity because there is no immune reaction to *and* or *too much*. Rather than a deadly infection, infarction is the pathological consequence of the *violence of positivity*. The limitless addition of the positive may convulse *being* (*Sein*). But it leads to a proliferation of *beings* (*Seiendes*), which is also violence.

Deleuze's protagonist is "the schizo": "As for the schizo, continually wandering about, migrating here, there, and everywhere as best he can, he plunges further and further into the realm of deterritorialization, reaching the furthest limits of the decomposition of the socius on the surface of his own body without organs. ... He scrambles all the codes and is the transmitter of the decoded flows of desire."[70] Deleuze idealizes the schizo to the wanderings of Lenz: "A schizophrenic out for a walk is a better model than a neurotic lying on the analyst's couch. ... Lenz's stroll, for example, as reconstructed by Buchner [sic]. ... Everything is a machine. Celestial machines, the stars or rainbows in the sky, alpine machines—all of them connected to those of his body. The continual whirr of machines. ... He does not live nature as nature, but as a process of production. There is no such thing as either man or nature now, only a process that produces the one within the other and couples the machines together. Producing-machines, desiring-machines everywhere, schizophrenic machines. ..."[71] The schizo is marked by his ability "to rearrange fragments continually in new and different patterns."[72] He possesses a death drive. Deleuze invokes Antonin Artaud: "The full body without organs is the unproductive, the sterile, the unengendered, the unconsumable. Antonin Artaud discovered this one day, finding himself with no shape or form whatsoever, right there where he was at that moment. The death instinct: that is its name, and death is not without a model. For desire desires death also. ..."[73] "... death is its motor," he says of the desiring-machine. They sabotage and destroy themselves, so that "its construction and the beginning of its destruction are indistinguishable."[74] The indistinguishability of construction and destruction, production and devastation, is a characteristic trait of schizophrenic machines, which are very similar to *capitalist machines.* Schizophrenic production, which fuses with destruction, does not differ meaningfully from unregulated capitalist production. Deleuze even establishes a significant correspondence between schizophrenia and capitalism: "The decoding of flows and the deterritorialization of the socius thus constitutes the most characteristic and the most important tendency of capitalism. It continually draws near to its limit, which is a genuinely schizophrenic limit. It tends, with all the strength at its command, to produce the schizo as the subject of the decoded flows on the body without organs. ..."[75]

According to Deleuze, capitalism produces not only schizophrenic traits but also paranoid ones. It oscillates between deterritorialization and reterritorialization. Deleuze diabolicizes only paranoid reterritorialization. He consistently maintains a positive attitude toward schizophrenic deterritorialization. Thus he suggests heightening the schizophrenic dissolution of boundaries against paranoid reterritorialization: "To go still further, that is, in the movement of the market, of decoding and deterritorialization?"[76] Schizophrenic deterritorialization leads to the rhizomatic proliferation of the same, to accumulation of the positive. Violence is not only the negativity of execution or exclusion but also the positivity of exorbitance and excess. Apparently, violence based on excess positivity isn't visible to Deleuze, and so he celebrates decoding and deterritorialization as liberation, ignoring their other side. The positive violence of excess is more calamitous than the negative violence of deficiency or deprivation. Deficiency naturally comes to an end when the point of saturation is reached, but excess knows no end.

Deleuze acquits schizophrenia of any diabolic characteristics. It is largely romanticized and idealized. He speaks of "a general and productive schizophrenia that has finally become happy."[77] The schizophrenic desiring-machines are compared with Tinguely's machines, whose elements are connected to each other without any functional logic: "In our present social order, the desiring-machine is tolerated only in its perverse forms, which is to say, on the fringes of the serious utilization of machines. ... But the desiring-machine's regime is not a generalized perversion, it is rather the opposite, a general and productive schizophrenia that has finally become happy. What Tinguely says of one of his own works applies to desiring-machines: *a truly joyous machine, by joyous I mean free.*"[78] The deterritorialized system whose elements communicate with each other despite a lack of any logical function or functioning ties, and which are related to each other despite their lack of relation, this *truly joyous system* shows no signs of rifts or fissures. Tinguely's machines elude all relations of function and purpose, but they form a continuum, a whole that is harmonious within itself. Their parts interlock playfully without any blockages. Somehow, they *relate*. They share a bond of friendship, which bestows proximity without relatedness. Because of this inner harmony, they run smoothly. True schizophrenia, in contrast, would cause disruptions and blockages. It is itself a form of compulsion. It makes things neither "joyous" nor "free."

Confronted with the negativity of the *other*, Hegel's spirit develops a paranoid hyperimmunity, which causes hyperencoding and hyperterritorialization. But Deleuze's countermodel of schizophrenic decoding and deterritorialization is also destructive and diabolic. Freed from all negativity, the schizomachine produces *violence of positivity*. It is like a nuclear reactor that *burns out* in the wake of uncontrolled chain reactions and overheating. Not all negativity is destructive. Not infrequently, forms of negativity such as hesitation, pausing, boredom, waiting, or rage prove constructive, though they are threatened with disappearance in the course of society's increasing positivization. As we know, computers do not hesitate. They lack the dimension of the *other*, which makes them *autistic calculation machines*. Thinking in the emphatic sense is also associated with negativity. Without negativity, thought would just be calculation. The schizophrenic "*and ... and ...*

and ..." lacks all negativity and leads to an accumulation of the positive. Only the negativity of a *constraint* allows cadence, rhythm, indeed *time itself,* to develop. Paranoid blockages as well as schizophrenic lack of constraint annihilate time.

12. THE VIOLENCE OF THE GLOBAL

According to Hardt and Negri, globalization has developed two opposing forces. On the one hand, it creates "empire," which establishes a decentralized, deterritorialized capitalist regime through constant control and perpetual conflict. On the other hand, it produces a "multitude," a body of singularities that communicate with each other via a network and act collectively. The multitude *opposes* empire from *within* empire. So Hardt and Negri have revamped class struggle. The violence generated by empire is interpreted as the violence of *exploiting the other:* "The multitude is the real productive force of our social world, whereas Empire is a mere apparatus of capture that lives only off the vitality of the multitude—as Marx would say, a vampire regime of accumulated dead labor that survives only by sucking off the blood of the living."[79]

Hardt and Negri pay too little consideration to political-economic realities, constructing their theoretical models on the basis of historically obsolete categories like class or class struggle. They define the "multitude" as a class: "One initial approach is to conceive the multitude as all those who work under the rule of capital and thus potentially as the class of those who refuse the rule of capital."[80] This talk of class only makes sense in the context of a plurality of classes that interact or compete with each other. But the multitude is basically the *only* class. After all, *everyone* who is part of the capitalist system belongs to it. It has no ruling class to struggle against. In empire, *everyone* is subjugated to the imperatives of the capitalist economy. Empire is not a ruling class that exploits the multitude as proletariat. Rather, the multitude exploits itself. Negri and Hardt do not recognize this *self-exploitation*. In empire, *no one* really rules. It represents the capitalist system, which encompasses *everyone*. Exploitation of the other does take place within it, but the basic method for maintaining the system is self-exploitation.

As Hardt and Negri themselves realize, "class is and can only be a collectivity that struggles in common."[81] Class requires an intense sense of belonging, which is the motivation for collective action. But contemporary society is characterized by the universal disappearance of this sense of belonging, of a *we*. And political apathy and indifference, paired with increasing infantilization of society, make collective action very unlikely. The globalized world is not populated by singularities committed to collective resistance against empire but rather by isolated and mutually antagonistic selves. Everyone involved in the capitalist production process is simultaneously victim and perpetrator. When perpetrator and victim are one, no resistance is possible. Hardt and Negri miss this particular topology of the global.

Social power arises only through collective action, from a we. But the ego-ification and atomization of society radically shrink the space available for collective action, hindering the formation of a counterforce that could truly challenge the capitalist order. *Socius* gives way to *solus*. It is not multitude but *solitude* that typifies contemporary social composition. Isolation doesn't generate power. Hardt and Negri fail to take this social development into account,[82] even pursuing an imaginary discourse that augurs a romantic communist revolution by the multitude.[83] The lack of a counterforce perpetuates the neoliberal economic order. It develops a strong appropriative energy, which absorbs everything and converts it into a capitalist formula.

After the fall of communism, capitalism no longer had an exterior that could jeopardize it in earnest. Even Islamic terrorism is not a manifestation of an equally matched base of power that could truly threaten the capitalist system. Capitalism can even absorb it and transform it into stabilizing systemic energies. Only an implosion of the system through overheating and overloading is conceivable. This implosive violence differs from explosive violence, which expands and conquers new territories through the violence of classic warfare. Explosive violence creates pressure outward. Owing to the lack of an exterior, implosive violence pushes inward. Destructive tensions and warping grow inside, causing the system to collapse into itself.

Violent conflicts taking place all over the world but lacking any solidarity are indiscriminately interpreted as a war against empire by Hardt and Negri. In reality, these conflicts don't necessarily have anything to do with neoliberalism. The violent conflicts listed by Hardt and Negri themselves do not point to any ideological solidarity or communal goal: the student revolt in Tiananmen Square, the racial unrest in Los Angeles in 1992, the Intifada, the uprising in Chiapas, the rail strikes in France. But Hardt and Negri themselves realize that no communication takes place between these struggles for resistance, which have neither a common language nor a common enemy,[84] but that does not lead them to recognize the insufficiency of their own thesis. Without communication there obviously cannot be any collective action, that is, any counterforce. Hardt and Negri simply impute a nonexistent communal intention to them. Lack of communication, they conjecture, is "a new type of communication," "a communication of singularities."[85] The struggles for resistance "do not link horizontally;" rather, each individual one "leaps vertically, directly to the virtual center of empire."[86]

Hardt and Negri argue counterfactually. In fact, society today is gripped by a general process of decline of the social, the common, and the communal. It is atomizing and particularizing noticeably. Contrary to this factual development comes the claim that the essence of contemporary production relations consists in "constructing cooperation and communicative commonalities," which would lead to a crisis of private property: "The concept of private property itself, understood as the exclusive right to use a good and dispose of all wealth that derives from the possession of it, becomes increasingly nonsensical. ..."[87] Contrary to their conclusion, today the communal is in a state of increasing decline. Nothing is sacred to the expanding privatization. The decline of the communal makes collective action ever less likely. Hardt and Negri overestimate the strength of the resistance against the capitalist neoliberal system. It is inherent in its constitution that the exploiters and the exploited are difficult to tell apart and that perpetrator and victim merge together. No unambiguous *opposition* forms, no clear front, that would require two separate camps, forces, or classes. This particular topology of violence escapes Hardt and Negri completely. They observe: "Although exploitation and domination are still experienced concretely, on the flesh of the multitude, they are nonetheless amorphous in such a way that it seems there is no place left to hide. If there is no longer a place that can be recognized as outside, we must be against in every place."[88] We must be against in every place, and yet it is unclear *what* it is we are resisting. And so the fictive determination of the multitude peters out into nothing. Hardt and Negri apparently do not recognize that in empire, combatants soon prove to be collaborators. Violence and exploitation are no longer counterparts because everyone exploits *themselves.* The perpetrator is also the victim. Exploitation by others gives way to self-exploitation. This exploitation takes place without domination, because it is performed in the name of freedom. Any counterpart that could be combated frontally is erased by this immanent violence.

The global capitalist-neoliberal system, which Hardt and Negri call "Empire," is actually the conflict-ridden interior of the world in which the human race wages war *with itself.* This war is total because it fuses completely with social relations and presents itself as freedom. The "distant roar of battle" that Foucault once heard sounding from disciplinary institutions has established itself as the keynote of society. War extends into the soul of every individual. One doesn't wage it against others but above all with oneself. In the face of this totality and immanence of war, classic resistance—which assumes a clear separation of interior and exterior, friend and enemy, rulership and subjugation—tilts at windmills.

The only possible way to oppose empire would be to mitigate the process that creates it, eliminating its diabolic sting. But the strategy that Hardt and Negri suggest would be problematic. They are of the opinion that it is neither possible nor desirable to reverse the process; rather, it must be accelerated and intensified. Thus they invoke Deleuze and Guattari: "Deleuze and Guattari argued that rather than resist capital's globalization, we have to accelerate the process. 'But which,' they ask, 'is the revolutionary path? ... — To withdraw from the world market? ... Or might it be to go in the opposite direction? To go still further, that is, in the movement of the market, of decoding and deterritorialization?' Empire can be effectively contested only on its own level of generality and by pushing the processes that it offers past their present limitations."[89] It would be devastating to go further and with more determination into the movement of the market and of capital. The *world* and the world market are not identical. The total commercialization of the *world* would be its violation. Commercialization represses and obliterates everything that isn't work, profit, capital, efficiency, and performance. The hysteria for production and performance and the hypertension of competition produce pathological symptoms of various kinds. The hypermobility of the global is like a total mobilization that poses as a peace accord. The attempt to accelerate and intensify the dynamic processes that govern empire beyond their current dimensions would have catastrophic consequences. Total burnout of the system would then be unavoidable.

13. *HOMO LIBER*

The state of exception is a state of extreme negativity because all positive norms are suspended within it. It ensues at the moment in which an exterior punctures the interior of a system and challenges its entirety. A negative tension between the interior and the exterior is essential for the state of exception. It confronts the immanence of a system with the transcendence of another, which threatens it. The negativity of the completely other induces a contraction within the system, causing it to quake. The establishment of the state of exception is a system's immunological reaction to a threat from the exterior.

The sovereign commands absolute power to suspend the current legal system. He embodies legislative power and violence, which maintains a relation to the legal order even outside it. Thus the sovereign need not be right in order to determine rights. By suspending the current legal order, the state of exception produces a lawless space in which absolute access to every individual is possible. According to Agamben, human life is only politicized by its inclusion in the power of sovereignty, that is, "only through an abandonment to an unconditional power of death."[90] Bare, mortal life and the power of sovereignty produce each other: "Contrary to our modern habit of representing the political realm in terms of citizens' rights, free will, and social contracts, from the point of view of sovereignty *only bare life is authentically political*."[91] "[L]ife exposed to death" is "the originary political element."[92] "[T]he *Urphänomen* of politics" is banishment, which produces "the bare life of *homo sacer*." Sovereignty and the bare life of *homo sacer* both stand at the outer limits of a system. In the eyes of the sovereign, all people are potential *homines sacri*.[93]

The fascination that Agamben's theory of sovereignty exerted doesn't attest to the fact that today the state of exception threatens to become the norm, as Agamben claims. To the contrary, it points to the fact that we now live in a society governed by an *excess of positivity* in which *a state of exception is no longer possible*. We often are fascinated by things that are on the brink of disappearing.[94] The state of exception is a *state of negativity*. It is only possible given an *intrusion of the other or exterior*. The positivization of society totalizes the normative state today by stripping it of all negativity and transcendence. It totalizes the interior, obliterating any exterior. Terror is produced not only by the transcendence of sovereignty but also by immanence. The terror of positivity might possibly be more catastrophic than the terror of negativity because it evades immune defense.

The society of sovereignty has long belonged to the past. Today, no one is politicized "through an abandonment to an unconditional power of death." There is no longer any exterior, no transcendence, no sovereignty of power to which one would be subjugated and exposed as an obedience-subject. Contemporary society is not a society of sovereignty. We now live in a society of achievement. The achievement-subject differs from the obedience-subject in that it is the *sovereign of itself*; as the entrepreneur of itself, it is *free*.

The achievement-subject is free from external authorities that would force it to work and exploit it. It is subjugated to no one, or only to itself. The loss of an external authority doesn't do away with the structure of compulsion. Freedom and compulsion merge. The achievement-subject devotes itself to the free compulsion for maximizing performance. It exploits itself. Self-exploitation is more efficient than exploitation by the other because it is accompanied by a misleading sense of freedom. The exploiter is also the exploited. In this case, exploitation takes place without domination. That is what makes self-exploitation so efficient. The capitalist system shifts from exploitation by the other to self-exploitation, from *should* to *can*, all *in order to accelerate.* As a result of its paradoxical freedom, the achievement-subject is at once perpetrator and victim, master and slave. Here, freedom and violence are indistinguishable. The achievement-subject, which pretends to be the sovereign of itself, *homo liber*, proves to be *homo sacer*. The sovereign of achievement society is at the same time the *homo sacer of itself*. Paradoxically, in the society of achievement, the sovereign and *homo sacer* also produce each other. But *they are identical*. That is the difference between reality and Agamben's theory of sovereignty.

Agamben adheres to the principle of negativity. In it, perpetrator and victim, sovereign and *homo sacer*, are clearly distinguished, also topologically. Sovereignty and the bare life of *homo sacer* both stand "at the outer limits of a system." Agamben's state of exception is a state of negativity. The *homines sacri* of achievement society, in contrast, live in a *totalized state of normality*, which is a *state of positivity*. Agamben completely misses the topological shift of violence that is the basis for the shift from the society of sovereignty to the society of achievement. The achievement society is characterized by the violence of positivity, which evades the immunological paradigm of negativity to which Agamben consistently adheres.

Muslim is a slang term for prisoners of a concentration camp who are completely enfeebled, emaciated, and apathetic. As *homines sacri* of a totalitarian society, they are at the outermost edge of an order, in a non-place. As the late modern *homo sacer*, the achievement-subject is *centrally located, directly at the center of an order.* Labor camps also are no longer located *on the outskirts.* Rather, every achievement-subject carries the camp *with it.* The center becomes indistinguishable from a non-place. The achievement-subject is prisoner and warden at once. It cannot defend itself from this violence because it is committed by itself. One has the creeping suspicion that the late-modern achievement-subject, with its psychic disorders like burnout and depression, is a *Muselmann* itself. *The history of violence culminates in this merging of victim and perpetrator, of master and slave, of freedom and violence.*

When Agamben notes that we all may possibly be virtual *homines sacri*, it is because we are all subject to sovereign banishment and absolute mortality. Agamben's social diagnosis contradicts all elements of contemporary society, which is no longer a society of sovereignty. The banishment that has made *homines sacri* of us all today is not the banishment of sovereignty but rather the *banishment of achievement.* The achievement-subject considers itself to be *free.* As *homo liber*, sovereign of itself, it is now subject to the *banishment of achievement*, turning itself into *homo sacer.* The sovereign of the achievement society is the *homo sacer of itself.*

Ehrenberg's theory of depression overlooks the systemic violence that is inherent in achievement society. Large portions of his analyses are psychologically and not economically or politically based. As a result, he doesn't recognize the capitalist relation of self-exploitation in the achievement-subject's disorders. According to Ehrenberg, depression arises only from the imperative to belong to oneself. Depression is the pathological expression of the failure of the late modern subject to become itself. Ehrenberg equates it with Nietzsche's sovereign man without recognizing that it is sovereign and *homo sacer* at once. For

Nietzsche it wouldn't be the sovereign man but rather the *last* man who exploits himself as his own slave.

Contrary to Ehrenberg's assumption, Nietzsche's sovereign man is actually a culturally critical countermodel to the exhausted, depressive achievement-subject. Thus he is presented as a man of leisure. Nietzsche would find hyperactivity repugnant. The "strong soul" conserves its "peace," "moves slowly," and feels "repugnance at the all too lively."[95] In *Thus Spoke Zarathustra*, Nietzsche writes: "All of you who are in love with hectic work and whatever is fast, new, strange—you find it hard to bear yourselves, your diligence is escape and the will to forget yourself. If you believed more in life, you would hurl yourself less into the moment. But you do not have enough content in yourselves for waiting—not even for laziness!"[96]

For Agamben, the power of sovereignty produces the sphere in which one can kill without committing murder. Life is sacred (*sacer*) when it is enclosed in this sphere of sovereignty. The sacredness of life originally meant "an unconditional subjection to a power of death. ..."[97] The production of the bare life of *homo sacer* is originally the work of sovereignty. *Homo sacer*'s life is bare because it exists outside the legal order and therefore can be killed at any time. The life of *homo sacer* of the achievement society is sacred and bare for entirely different reasons. It is bare because it has been stripped of any transcendence of *value*, reduced to the immanence of the vital functions and performance, which must be maximized with all available means. Through its own inner logic, the achievement society develops into a *doping society*. Life reduced to its bare vital functions is a life that must be kept *healthy* at any cost. Health is the new goddess of today.[98] It is what makes *bare* life sacred. The *homines sacri* of the achievement society have another characteristic that sets them apart from those of the society of sovereignty: they are impossible to kill. Their lives are like those of the undead. They are too alive to *die* and too dead to *live*.

Notes

INTRODUCTION

1. When Jan Philipp Reemtsma speaks of the aversion to violence and the delegitimation of violence in the modern, he has only raw, corporeal violence in mind. He does not take note of systemic violence or more subtle forms of violence. See Jan Philipp Reemtsma, *Vertrauen und Gewalt* (Hamburg: Hamburger Edition, 2008).

PART I

1. Ovid, *Metamorphoses*, bk. 6, trans. Rolfe Humphries (Bloomington: Indiana University Press, 1960), 151–152, ll. 681–691.

2. Linda Günther and Michael Oberweis, eds., *Inszenierungen des Todes* (Berlin: Europäischer Universitätsverlag, 2006), 37.

3. Sigmund Freud, *Civilization and Its Discontents*, trans. James Strachey (New York: Norton, 1961), 84.

4. Sigmund Freud, letter to Albert Einstein, September 1932 (http://users.humboldt.edu/jwpowell/FreudEinstein_WhyWar.pdf).

5. See Sigmund Freud, "The Economic Problem of Masochism," in *The Standard Edition of the Complete Psychological Works of Sigmund Freud*, trans. James Strachey, vol. 19 (London: Hogarth Press, 1961), 159–170.

6. René Girard, *Violence and the Sacred*, trans. Patrick Gregory (Baltimore: Johns Hopkins University Press, 1977), 145ff.

7. Girard, *Violence and the Sacred*, 145ff.

8. René Girard, *Things Hidden Since the Foundation of the World*, trans. Stephen Bann and Michael Metteer (Stanford: Stanford University Press, 1987), 12.

9. Girard accuses Plato of not having recognized the true reason for the prohibition of mimesis in "primitive" cultures: "If Plato mistrusts art it is because it is a form of mimesis, and not the reverse. He shares with primitive peoples a terror of mimesis. ... Yet Plato is also deceived by mimesis because he cannot succeed in understanding his fear. ... Plato never relates conflict to acquisitive mimesis, that is, with the object that the two mimetic rivals attempt to wrest from one another because they designate it as desirable to one another" (Girard, *Things Hidden Since the Foundation of the World*, 15). Girard's critique of Plato is completely unfounded. He completely misses the metaphysical motivations of the Platonic critique of mimesis. For Plato, mimesis is forbidden, on the one hand because it is a mere representation of an idea and therefore displays a deficiency of being. On the other hand, mimetic behavior is objectionable because it poses a danger to identity, because those who imitate become what they imitate. They do not remain identical to themselves. Any polymorphism is objectionable to Plato because the good is "one-formed" (*monoeides*). Ultimately, Plato's prohibition of mimesis is a prohibition of transformation. It corresponds to the metaphysical dictate for identity.

10. For other examples of ritualistic killing, see Walter Burkert, *Homo Necans* (Berkeley, CA: University of California Press, 1983). Burkert is also of the opinion that one kills in order to overcome death.

11. Girard, *Violence and the Sacred*, 15.

12. Ibid., 7–8.

13. See Girard, *Violence and the Sacred*, 19: "the ability of violence to move from one object to another ... is hidden from sight by the awesome machinery of ritual."

14. Ibid., 259: The role of the religious is to eliminate "the threat this violence poses for human society."

15. For Hegel, sacrifice is anything but a violence-preventing measure arising out of fear of the destruction of social order. Rather, he defines it as a "joyous action." Accordingly, the mortal subject relinquishes what is proper to it in favor of the absolute. A sacrifice is an "act of testifying that I have nothing peculiar to myself but that I relinquish it in thinking of myself in relation to the Absolute." G. W. F. Hegel, *Lectures on the Philosophy of Religion*, trans. E. B. Speirs and J. Burdon Sanderson (London: Kegan Paul, Trench, Trübner & Co., 1895), 252.

16. Friedrich Nietzsche, *The Anti-Christ*, trans. H. L. Mencken, vol. 1, *The Anti-Christ*, sec. 16 (New York: Knopf, 1920), 27.

17. The behavior of a society is passive-immunological if it administers violence to itself in a weakened form in order to immunize itself against it. See Girard, *Violence and the Sacred*, 305: "And what about the modern practice of immunization and inoculation? ... The physician inoculates the patient with a minute amount of the disease, just as, in the course of the rites, the community is injected with a minute amount of violence, enabling it to ward off an attack of full-fledged violence. The analogies abound."

18. E. S. Craighill Handy, *Polynesian Religion* (Honolulu: Bernice P. Bishop Museum, 1927), 31. Baudler traces archaic deadly violence to the attempt to reach "predator status" and to leave "prey status." But the struggle for predator status does not account for the *capitalist* economy of mana. See G. Baudler, *Ursünde Gewalt* (Ostfildern: Patmos Verlag, 2001).

19. Pierre Clastres, *Archeology of Violence*, trans. Jeanine Herman (New York: Semiotext(e), 1994), 90.

20. The king himself is subject to higher powers: "The king rules when the full moon is shining; during the waning moon, he withdraws into seclusion. But if the stars have completed

their multiyear rotation, in order to be born anew, the priests strangle the king in a mineshaft along with his women. When the moon waxes again, a new ruler is elevated to the throne." Wolfgang Binde, *Tabu* (Bern: Verlag Paul Hapt, 1954), 76–77. The king of archaic society is anything but an all-powerful ruler: "It was said he lived in a hut in the dark; he would die if he saw the sun or moon. As was reported from the mouth of the Congo, the king is tied to his chair, where he even sleeps sitting upright at night. The king rules and is shackled and dies according to the rules of the all-powerful, which has its own time" (Binde, *Tabu*, 77).

21. See Claude Lévi-Strauss, *The Elementary Structures of Kinship*, trans. James Harle Bell, Johne Richard von Sturmer, and Rodney Needham (Boston: Beacon Press, 1969), 68: "There is a link, a continuity, between hostile relations and the provision of reciprocal prestations. Exchanges are peacefully resolved wars, and wars are the result of unsuccessful transactions."

22. Clastres, *Archeology of Violence*, 163.

23. Ibid., 165–166.

24. Archaic society *cannot* produce a power structure like the state. Clastres mistakes desire for ability when he writes: "To hold power is to exercise it; to exercise it is to dominate those over whom it is being exercised: this is precisely what primitive societies do not want (did not want). ..." (Clastres, *Archeology of Violence*, 91).

25. See Baudler, *Ursünde Gewalt*, 115.

26. Aristotle points to the fact that pure accumulation of capital is objectionable because it is concerned with mere life and not with the good life: "Consequently some people suppose that it is the function of household management to increase property, and they are continually under the idea that it is their duty to be either safeguarding their substance in money or increasing it to an unlimited amount. The cause of this

state of mind is that their interests are set upon life but not upon the good life; as therefore the desire for life is unlimited, they also desire without limit the means productive of life." Aristotle, *Aristotle in 23 Volumes*, vol. 21, trans. H. Rackham (Cambridge, MA: Harvard University Press, 1944), 1257b.

27. Sigmund Freud, *Reflections on War and Death*, trans. A. A. Brill and Alfred B. Kuttner (New York: Moffat, Yard & Co., 1918), 72.

28. Ibid., 71.

29. Sigmund Freud, *The Ego and the Id*, trans. Joan Riviere (London: Hogarth Press, 1949), 40, 45.

30. Ibid., 80.

31. Ibid., 77.

32. Ibid., 69.

33. Sigmund Freud, "Repression," in *The Standard Edition of the Complete Works of Sigmund Freud*, vol. 14, trans. and ed. James Strachey (London: Hogarth Press, 1957), 146.

34. The translation of Freud's term *Besetzung* is problematic in English. James Strachey (whose translations of Freud remain nearly canonical) rendered the term *cathexis*. Later scholars objected to this translation as unnatural, unlike its commonly used, multivalent German counterpart. Alternative translations such as "investment," "charge," and "occupation" have been used since the late 1980s. However, none of these is as unambiguous (or at least as easy to look up) as *cathexis*, and all of them still sit a bit awkwardly in the English sentences they are supposed to improve. Using *cathexis* also allowed me to maintain continuity with citations, for which I believe Strachey's translation is worth its concomitant difficulties.—Translator.

35. Sigmund Freud, "Mourning and Melancholia," in *The Standard Edition of the Complete Works of Sigmund Freud*, vol. 14, 248–249.

36. Ibid.," 251.

37. Ibid.," 84.

38. Immanual Kant, *The Metaphysics of Morals*, trans. Mary Gregor (Cambridge: Cambridge University Press, 1996), 189.

39. Ibid., 189.

40. Ibid., 189 (footnote).

41. Kant, *Critique of Practical Reason*, trans. Mary Gregor, rev. ed. (Cambridge: Cambridge University Press, 2015), 90.P. 239.

42. Richard Sennett, *The Fall of Public Man* (New York: Norton, 1974), 324–325.

43. Ibid., 335.

44. Freud, *The Ego and the Id*, 24.

45. Alain Ehrenberg, *The Weariness of the Self: Diagnosing the History of Depression in the Contemporary Age*, trans. Enrico Caouette, Jacob Homel, David Homel, and Don Winkler (Montreal: McGill–Queen's University Press, 2010), 218.

46. Ibid., 232: "Depression portrays for all of us the style of the uncontrollable in the age of limitless possibilities. We can manipulate our bodily and mental nature, we can push back our limits by all sorts of means, but this manipulation won't save us from anything. Constraints and freedoms change, but that 'irreducible part' is not diminished."

47. Ibid., 230.

48. Ibid., 218.

49. Ibid., 219.

50. Forms of closure generate a lack of flexibility that would hinder the acceleration of the capitalist production process. The achievement-subject exploits itself most effectively when it remains open to everything, that is, by being flexible.

51. Ehrenberg, *The Weariness of the Self*, 10.

52. Ibid., 215.

53. Axel Honneth writes in his foreword to the German edition: "In his estimation, there is the threat that the psychic structure of the subject today forms without fundamental friction with social challenges and inner conflict with society, which are alarmingly the prerequisites for civil democracy; after all, its vitality depends fundamentally on the engagement of its citizens, who are only capable of taking controversial positions and engaging in the conflict-strewn process of the shaping of public opinion if they have succeeded in gathering experience in intrapsychic conflict through their own personal development, which would in some sense provide them with a horizon of understanding in the face of social dissent." Axel Honneth, introduction to *Das erschöpfte Selbst*, by Alain Ehrenberg (Frankfurt am Main: Suhrkamp Verlag, 2008), 9.

54. Ehrenberg, *The Weariness of the Self*, 205–206.

55. Ehrenberg traces the auto-aggression that is characteristic of depression back to the unlocalizable quality of guilt and responsibility: "Instead of struggles between social groups, individual competition affects people. ... We are witnessing a double phenomenon: increasing universality (globalization), which is abstract, and acute personalization, which is felt more concretely. ... It is much more difficult to demand justice in this context or to pin the responsibility for a situation that has victimized us on an adversary we can name. ... Resentment turns towards oneself (depression is an attack on the self) or towards a scapegoat. ..." (Ehrenberg, *The Weariness of the Self*, 223–224). Faced with the complexity of the social-economic situation, which do not allow clear attribution of guilt, it is indeed conceivable that one directs resentment at oneself, but this self-reproach differs significantly from the auto-aggression that often leads to suicide.

56. See Carl Schmitt, *The Concept of the Political*, trans. George Schwab (Chicago: University of Chicago Press, 1996), 27: The

enemy is "the other, the stranger ... existentially something different and alien, so that in the extreme case conflicts with him are possible. These can neither be decided by a previously determined general norm nor by the judgement of a disinterested and therefore neutral third party."

57. Ibid., 67.

58. Ibid., 26.

59. Ibid., 46. [The English translation of *The Concept of the Political* cited here elides certain aspects of the original. A full translation of the passage cited by Han would read: "The real friend-and-enemy grouping is existentially so strong and decisive that the nonpolitical antithesis, at precisely the moment at which it becomes political, pushes aside and subordinates its hitherto purely religious, purely economic, purely critical criteria and motives to the completely new, unique conditions and conclusions of the political situation at hand, which, viewed from that 'purely' religious or 'purely' economic or any other 'pure' starting point, are often insignificant or 'irrational.'"—Translator]

60. Ibid., 45.

61. Carl Schmitt, *Theory of the Partisan*, trans. G. L. Ulmen (New York: Telos, 2007), 61.

62. Schmitt, *The Concept of the Political*, 67.

63. Ibid., 39.

64. Ibid., 39.

65. See Carl Schmitt, *Political Theology*, trans. George Schwab (Chicago: University of Chicago Press, 2005), 12: "Because the exception is different from anarchy and chaos, order in the juristic sense still prevails even if it is not of the ordinary kind. The existence of the state is undoubted proof of its superiority over the validity of the legal norm. The decision frees itself from all normative ties and becomes in the true sense absolute."

66. Schmitt, *The Concept of the Political*, 49.

67. Ibid., 46.

68. Ibid., 49.

69. Martin Heidegger, *Being and Time*, trans. Joan Stambaugh (Albany: SUNY Press, 1996), 119. [In this passage, I have rendered Heidegger's "Man" as "the 'they,'" drawing on Macquarrie and Robinson's translation (Oxford: Blackwell, 1962). Other translations of the term include "the Anyone" (Blattner, *Heidegger's* Being and Time: *A Reader's Guide* [London: Continuum, 2006]) or "the one" (Blattner, *Heidegger's Temporal Idealism* [Cambridge: Cambridge University Press, 1999], John Haugeland, *Dasein Disclosed* [Cambridge, MA: Harvard University Press, 2013])—Translator.]

70. Martin Heidegger, "The Self-Assertion of the German University," *Review of Metaphysics* 38, no. 3 (1985): 475.

71. Schmitt, *The Concept of the Political*, 71–72.

72. Carl Schmitt, *Political Romanticism*, trans. Guy Oakes (New Brunswick, NJ: Transaction Publishers, 2011), 19.

73. Ibid., 128.

74. Schmitt, *The Concept of the Political*, 35.

75. Carl Schmitt, *The Nomos of the Earth*, trans. G. L. Ulmen (New York: Telos, 2006), 42–43.

76. Carl Schmitt, *Land und Meer* (Cologne: Klett-Cotta, 1981), 7.

77. Carl Schmitt, *Ex Captivitate Salus* (Berlin: Duncker & Humblot, 2002), 89.

78. G. W. F. Hegel, *Elements of the Philosophy of Right*, trans. H. B. Nisbet (Cambridge: Cambridge University Press, 1991), 289 (footnote to sec. 268).

79. Walter Benjamin, "Critique of Violence," in *Reflections*, trans. Edmund Jephcott (New York: Shocken Books, 1986), 295.

80. Ibid.," 294.

81. Hesiod, *Works and Days*, in *The Homeric Hymns and Homerica*, trans. Hugh G. Evelyn-White (Cambridge, MA: Harvard University Press, 1914), ll. 274–280. Agamben also cites this verse, but without recognizing the significant difference between violence and right. See Agamben, *Homo Sacer*, trans. Daniel Heller-Roazen (Stanford, CA: Stanford University Press, 1998), 24.

82. Benjamin, "Critique of Violence," 296–297.

83. Ibid., 288.

84. Ibid., 288.

85. Ibid., 288–289.

86. Ibid., 289.

87. Ibid., 293.

88. Ibid., 290.

89. Ibid., 290.

90. Ibid., 289.

91. Ibid., 293.

92. Ibid., 297.

93. Moses *interprets* the unusual death of the company of Korah as a sign that God had chosen him: "By this you shall know that the Lord has sent me to do all these works, for I have not done them of my own will. If these men die naturally like all men, or if they are visited by the common fate of all men, then the Lord has not sent me. But if the Lord creates a new thing, and the earth opens its mouth and swallows them up with all that belongs to them, and they go down alive into the pit, then you will understand that these men have rejected the Lord" (Num 16:28–30 NKJV).

94. Benjamin, "Critique of Violence," 297–298.

95. Ibid., 297.

96. Ibid., 300.

97. Giorgio Agamben, *State of Exception*, trans. Kevin Attell (Chicago: University of Chicago Press, 2005), 64.

98. Agamben, *Homo Sacer*, 29.

99. Aristotle, *Politics*, in *Aristotle in 23 Volumes*, vol. 21, trans. H. Rackham (Cambridge, MA: Harvard University Press, 1944), 1252b.

100. Aristotle, *Nichomachean Ethics*, in *Aristotle in 23 Volumes*, vol. 19, trans. H. Rackham (Cambridge, MA: Harvard University Press, 1934), 1155a.

101. Aristotle, *Politics*, 1262b.

102. Ibid., 1295b.

103. Ibid., 1281a.

104. Thus, purely economic organization that is oriented only toward profit cannot build a community. It lacks the political dimension to do so. As such, the economic system, whose binary code is "profit/loss," is blind to the common good. This example demonstrates the true essence of the political.

105. From the perspective of his political understanding, Aristotle rejects any political constitution that is aligned toward war and domination (*Politics*, 1333b). "[A] lover of war" is "by nature unsocial" (*Politics*, 1253a). Politics doesn't mean cutting off the other as an enemy, but rather mediation and consolidation. War is a political act only if it is waged for the sake of peace (*Politics*, 1333a).

106. Agamben, *State of Exception*, 88.

107. Agamben, *Homo Sacer*, 65.

108. Thomas Hobbes, "The Citizen," in *Man and Citizen,* trans. Charles T. Wood, T. S. K. Scott-Craig, and Bernard Gert (Cambridge, MA: Hackett Publishing Co., 1991), 170.

109. Thomas Hobbes, *Leviathan* (London, 1651) (https://ebooks.adelaide.edu.au/h/hobbes/thomas/h68l/complete.html).

110. Hobbes, *Leviathan*, 18.6.

111. The German word *Gewalt* means both violence and authority or power. This dual meaning is particularly important in this passage.—Translator.

112. Giorgio Agamben, *Means without End*, trans. Vincenzo Binetti and Cesare Casarino (Minneapolis: University of Minnesota Press, 2000), 103.

113. Ibid., 107.

114. Ibid. This claim completely contradicts the fact that a good number of U.S. soldiers were sentenced to life in prison after being convicted of brutal crimes against Iraqi civilians.

115. Ibid., 112.

116. Ibid., 96. Although, like Aristotle, Agamben connects speech with politics, speech is robbed of its political dimension because it is once again reduced to its factuality. Aristotle doesn't trace the political dimension of language back to the *factum loquendi*. Rather, language is *logos*. Humans, capable of speaking, are beings gifted with reason (*zoon logon echon*). This fundamental proximity of language and logos makes human beings the *zoon politikon*. It is not the factuality of being-in-language but rather the logicality of language that lends it its political essence. Its *logicality* gives humans the ability to tell right from wrong, just from unjust.

117. Jean Baudrillard, *The Transparency of Evil*, trans. James Benedict (London: Verso, 2009), 127.

118. Giorgio Agamben, *The Kingdom and the Glory*, trans. Lorenzo Chiesa and Matteo Mandarini (Stanford, CA: Stanford University Press, 2011), xii.

119. Ibid., 256.

120. Martin Heidegger, *Veröffentlichte Schriften 1910–1976*, vol. 16 (Frankfurt am Main: Verlag Vittorio Klostermann, 2000), 563.

121. Martin Heidegger, *Briefwechsel mit E. Blochmann* (Marbach am Neckar: Deutsche Schillerges, 1989), 23.

122. Hannah Arendt, *Denktagebuch*, vol. 1 (Munich: Piper Verlag, 2002), 276.

123. See Augustine, *Epistolam Ioannis, Tractatus*, 8, 10.

124. Augustine, *Sermo Lambot* 27, 3.

125. Aristotle, *Nichomachean Ethics*, 1166a.

126. Ibid., 1166b.

127. Heinrich von Kleist, *Penthesilea,* trans. Joel Agee (New York: Harper Perennial, 2000), 137.

128. Friedrich Nietzsche, *Kritische Gesamtausgabe,* sec. 5, vol. 2 (New York: de Gruyter, 1967), 448.

129. See Niklas Luhmann, *Die Wirtschaft der Gesellschaft* (Frankfurt am Main: Suhrkamp, 1988), 257: "Symbols merge the disparate into a single unit in such a way that their togetherness is recognizable from both sides, without blending them or dissolving their difference." From this point of view, money is a symbolic medium, and so is power. But, as Luhmann notes, a *symbolon* implies a *diabolon.*

PART II

1. Johan Galtung, "Violence, Peace & Peace Research," *Journal of Peace Research* 6, no. 3 (1969), 170–171.

2. Ibid., 169.

3. Ibid., 177.

4. Pierre Bourdieu, "Die männliche Herrschaft," in *Ein alltägliches Spiel* (Frankfurt am Main: Suhrkamp, 1997), 165.

5. Slavoj Žižek, *Violence* (New York: Picador, 2008), 36.

6. Ibid., 9.

7. Ibid., 15.

8. Ibid., 93.

9. Ibid., 103.

10. Ibid., 146.

11. Michel Foucault, *The History of Sexuality*, vol. 1, *An Introduction*, trans. Robert Hurley (New York: Pantheon, 1978), 136.

12. Ibid., 136.

13. Ibid., 139.

14. Ibid.,140.

15. Ibid., 144.

16. Ibid., 139.

17. Ibid., 141.

18. The fact that the populace now appears as sovereign does not imply a simple shift of power but rather a disempowerment of power, whose basic feature is hierarchy. Democratic communication oriented toward consensus is no longer a communication of power.

19. Foucault, *The History of Sexuality*, vol. 1, *An Introduction*, 92.

20. Ibid., 92.

21. Ibid., 94.

22. Michel Foucault, "The Subject and Power," *Critical Inquiry* 8, no. 4 (Summer 1982): 788.

23. Foucault, *The History of Sexuality*, vol. 1, *An Introduction*, 137.

24. Ibid., 137.

25. Foucault primarily conceives of torture as a process of truth. Of course, it is a "duel" between the torturer and the victim that is carried out for the sake of the truth. Torture, according to Foucault, was "certainly cruel, but it was not savage. It was a regulated practice, obeying a well-defined procedure. ..." Foucault is keen to pursue the bureaucracy of martyrdom and the organization of torture, completely losing sight of the aspect of violence: "... the various stages, their duration, the instruments used, the length of ropes and the heaviness of the weights used, the number of interventions made by the interrogating magistrate, all this was, according to the

different local practices, carefully codified. ... Torture was a strict judicial game." Michel Foucault, *Discipline and Punish*, trans. Alan Sheridan (New York: Vintage, 1977), 40. Foucault directs his attention only to the administrative and bureaucratic rigor, which he believes characterizes modern power technologies. The torturer becomes a bureaucrat of pain who carries out his duties in the name of the truth. Actually, torture follows the economy of pleasure more than that of the truth. In the end, it doesn't come down to the confession. Language itself is often emptied of all communicative function and used as a truncheon.

26. Foucault, *The History of Sexuality*, vol. 1, *An Introduction*, 138–139.

27. Giorgio Agamben, *Homo Sacer: Sovereign Power and Bare Life*, trans. Daniel Heller-Roazen (Stanford, CA: Stanford University Press, 1998), 10.

28. Foucault, *Discipline and Punish*, 308.

29. Baudrillard, *The Transparency of Evil*, 121.

30. Ibid., 71.

31. Ibid., 69.

32. Ibid., 83.

33. Jean Baudrillard, interview, *Der Spiegel*, January 15, 2002.

34. Jean Baudrillard, *Der Geist des Terrorismus* (Vienna: Passagen, 2002), 85.

35. Ibid., 86.

36. Baudrillard, *The Spirit of Terrorism*, trans. Chris Turner, rev. ed. (London: Verso, 2003), 15.

37. Baudrillard, *Der Geist des Terrorismus*, 63.

38. Baudrillard, *The Spirit of Terrorism*, 94.

39. Ibid., 94.

40. Baudrillard, *Der Geist des Terrorismus*, 54.

41. Arthur Schnitzler, *Aphorismen und Betrachtungen* (Frankfurt am Main: S. Fischer Verlag, 1967), 177–178. Baudrillard concurs with Schnitzler's vision of an ontological or even a cosmic necessity for the general demise of life. He believes that the secret fate of every individual is to destroy the other, though not through aggression or the evil intention to do the other harm but rather simply because of the fact of its own existence. Existence as such is already violence. The one's "life purpose" means that the other must perish, although neither recognizes that their survival is linked to the existence of the other.

42. Martin Heidegger, *On the Way to Language*, trans. Peter D. Hertz (New York: Harper & Row, 1971), 57.

43. Peter Handke, *Am Felsfenster morgens* (Salzburg: Residenz, 1998), 336.

44. Freud writes in a letter to Wilhelm Fließ: "As you know, I am working on the assumption that our psychic mechanism has come into being by a process of stratification: the material present in the form of memory traces being subjected from time to time to a *rearrangement* in accordance with fresh circumstances—to a *retranscription*. Thus what is essentially new about my theory is the thesis that memory is present not once but several times over, that it is laid down in various kinds of indications." Sigmund Freud, *The Complete Letters of Sigmund Freud to Wilhelm Fliess*, trans. Jeffrey Moussaieff Masson (Cambridge, MA: Belknap Press of Harvard University Press, 1985), 207.

45. Carl Schmitt, *The Crisis of Parliamentary Democracy*, trans. Ellen Kennedy (Cambridge, MA: MIT Press, 1988), 37–38.

46. Carl Schmitt, *Roman Catholicism and Political Form*, trans. G. L. Ulmen (Westport, CT: Greenwood Press, 1996), 34.

47. Ibid., 34.

48. Jean Baudrillard, *Fatal Strategies*, trans. Phil Beitchman and W. G. J. Niesluchowski, new ed. (Los Angeles: Semiotext(e), 2008), 51.

49. Jean Baudrillard, *Fatal Strategies*, in *Selected Writings* (Stanford, CA: Stanford University Press, 1988), 188.

50. Jean Baudrillard, *The Divine Left*, trans. David L. Sweet (Los Angeles: Semiotext(e), 2014), 123.

51. If only the symbolic side of language is taken into consideration, it leads to naive idealism. For Hannah Arendt, language is understanding per se. Thus she unites the linguistic and the political. The essence of the political is negotiating together, which is based on speaking to each other. Violence, in contrast, is speechless and silent. See Hannah Arendt, *On Revolution* (New York: Penguin, 1990), 19. Its silence alone makes it only peripherally political. Where language ends, so does politics. Arendt ignores the diabolic side of language, which lends language to violence and blocks negotiations.

52. Nietzsche also assumes an originary proximity of word and violence. Communicating oneself, he says, means "extending one's violence over the other. ..." Friedrich Nietzsche, *Nachgelassene Fragmente 1882–1884, Kritische Gesamtausgabe*, sec. 7, vol. 1 (Berlin: de Gruyter, 1998), 306. As a manifestation of will, the message expresses itself as the overpowering of others. To speak is to injure. The first symbol is "the (often painful) impression of one will upon another will." The "injuries of the other" distinguish the "symbolic language of the stronger." Understanding takes place directly as the sensation of sorrow and pain. If we extend Nietzsche's line of thought, symbols were originally scars. The logic of violence is continued in grammar. Conjugation is a violent subjugation of the other through declension and inflection. The subject and object of a sentence behave in relationship to each other like master and slave. But if language is considered only in terms of its symbolic side, conjugation would no longer be violent declension but

rather adjusting and adapting to each other. Inflection would be viewed in terms of flexibility.

53. The current interest in linguistic violence certainly isn't based on the fact that it is particularly virulent today. Rather, it is due to the fact that today we refuse all forms of physical violence, so that the *violence of negativity* is now possible only in the medium of language. Thus the current focus on linguistic violence is not prospective but rather retrospective and nostalgic.

54. Microblogging and social networks such as Facebook can absolutely play a constructive role in a *society of negativity*, such as a dictatorship. They make it possible to evade the controlling power to organize protests, as we can observe in the Arab world today. But in a *society of positivity* such as the West, they mutate and positivize themselves into exhibition spaces for the hypertrophied *I-am*.

55. René Descartes, *Principles of Philosophy*, in *The Philosophical Writings of Descartes*, vol. 1, trans. John Cottingham, Robert Stoothoff, and Dugald Murdoch (Cambridge: Cambridge University Press, 1985), 194–195.

56. Zygmunt Bauman, *Consuming Life* (Cambridge: Polity Press, 2007), 17.

57. Heidegger, *On the Way to Language*, 32.

58. See Emmanuel Lévinas, *Entre Nous*, trans. Michael B. Smith and Barbara Harshav (New York: Columbia University Press, 1998), 144. "My being-in-the-world or my 'place in the sun,' my home—have they not been a usurpation of places which belong to the others already oppressed or starved by me, expelled by me into a third world: a repelling, an exclusion, an exile, a spoliation, a killing."

59. Emmanuel Lévinas, "Ethics as First Philosophy," in *The Levinas Reader*, ed. Seán Hand (Oxford: Oxford University Press, 1989), 82.

60. Emmanuel Lévinas, *Otherwise Than Being or Beyond Essence*, trans. Alphonso Lingis (Pittsburgh, PA: Duquesne, 1998), 85. Subjectivity "is an irreplaceable oneself. Not strictly speaking an ego set up in the nominative in its identity, but first constrained to. ... It is set up as it were in the accusative form, from the first responsible and not being able to slip away."

61. Lévinas, *Otherwise Than Being or Beyond Essence*, 15.

62. Michel Serres, *Malfeasance*, trans. Anne-Marie Feenberg-Dibon (Stanford, CA: Stanford University Press, 2011), 69–70.

63. Ibid., 85.

64. Ibid., 24.

65. Ibid., 51.

66. Baudrillard, *The Transparency of Evil*, 35.

67. Gilles Deleuze and Félix Guattari, *Anti-Oedipus*, trans. Robert Hurley, Mark Seem, and Helen R. Lane (Minneapolis: University of Minnesota Press, 1983), 10.

68. See Gilles Deleuze and Félix Guattari, *A Thousand Plateaus*, trans. Brian Massumi (Minneapolis: University of Minnesota Press, 1987), 7: "[A]ny point of a rhizome can be connected to anything other, and must be. This is very different from the tree or root, which plots a point, fixes an order."

69. Ibid., 25.

70. Deleuze and Guattari, *Anti-Oedipus*, 35.

71. Ibid., 9.

72. Ibid., 7.

73. Ibid., 8.

74. Félix Guattari, *Chaosophy*, trans. David L. Sweet, Jarred Becker, and Taylor Adkins (Los Angeles: Semiotext(e), 2009), 105.

75. Deleuze and Guattari, *Anti-Oedipus*, 34.

76. Ibid., 239.

77. Guattari, *Chaosophy*, 109.

78. Giorgio Agamben, *Means without End*, trans. Vincenzo Binetti and Cesare Casarino (Minneapolis: University of Minnesota Press, 2000), 96.

79. Michael Hardt and Antonio Negri, *Empire* (Cambridge, MA: Harvard University Press, 2000), 62.

80. Michael Hardt and Antonio Negri, *Multitude* (New York: Penguin, 2004), 106.

81. Hardt and Negri, *Multitude*, 104.

82. Lacking clear resistance strategies, Hardt and Negri avail themselves of mythical-utopian incantations: They invoke Assisi and Augustine. Plotinus is also quoted: "'Let us flee then to the beloved Fatherland': this is the soundest counsel. ... The Fatherland to us is There whence we have come, and There is the Father. What then is our course, what the manner of our flight? This is not a journey for the feet; the feet bring us only from land to land; nor need you think of a coach or ship to carry you away; all this order of things you must set aside and refuse to see: you must close the eyes and call instead upon another vision which is to be waked within you..." (Hardt and Negri, *Empire*, 396).

83. Thus, their book closes with a romantic glorification of communism: "Once again in postmodernity we find ourselves in Francis [of Assisi]'s situation, posing against the misery of power the joy of being. This is a revolution that no power will control—because biopower and communism, cooperation and revolution remain together, in love, simplicity, and also innocence. This is the irrepressible lightness and joy of being communist" (Hardt and Negri, *Empire*, 413).

84. See: Hardt and Negri, *Empire*, 56. "We must admit, in fact, that even when trying to individuate the real novelty of these situations, we are hampered by the nagging impression that these struggles are always already old, outdated, and

anachronistic. The struggles at Tiananmen Square spoke a language of democracy that seemed long out of fashion; the guitars, headbands, tents, and slogans all looked like a weak echo of Berkeley in the 1960s. The Los Angeles riots, too, seemed like an aftershock of the earthquake of racial conflicts that shook the United States in the 1960s. The strikes in Paris and Seoul seemed to take us back to the era of the mass factory worker, as if they were the last gasp of a dying working class."

85. Ibid., 57.

86. Ibid., 58.

87. Ibid., 302.

88. Ibid., 211.

89. Ibid., 206.

90. Agamben, *Homo Sacer*, 56.

91. Ibid., 64.

92. These two short quoted passages are from Agamben, *Homo Sacer*, 59.—Translator.

93. *Homo sacer* is a person who has been expelled from society because of violation of a divine command. For example, anyone who moved a boundary marker was subject to the vengeance of *Jupiter terminalis*, the god of borders. That person could be killed without incurring punishment. However, *homo sacer* passed through several historical stages. In the laws of the Twelve Tables, composed in the fifth century B.C., anyone who violated the sacrosanctity of the plebeian tribune was *sacer*. The plebs resurrected this old, originally religious practice to secure their power. Agamben completely ignores the historical development of *homo sacer*, limiting *sacratio* to the time of plebian rulership. He erroneously traces *sacratio* back to the plebeian tribune's *potestas sacrosancta*. In doing so, he erases the religious origins of *sacratio*, conflating it with the power of sovereignty. The renowned legal historian Emil Brunnenmeister writes: "Sacer ... was not a worldly

status, it was exclusively divine banishment. That alone slowly developed into worldly banishment." Emil Brunnenmeister, *Das Tötungsverbrechen im altrömischen Recht* (Leipzig: Duncker & Humblot, 1887), 153. Furthermore, to substantiate his thesis, Agamben creates a contradiction in the figure of *homo sacer* that does not exist in reality. He suggests that it's impossible that *homo sacer* belongs to the religious arena because one is allowed to kill *homo sacer*, whereas it is forbidden to harm the rest of the sacred things (*res sacrae*). The possibility of death by human hand does not purge *homo sacer* from the religious because it was assumed that divine vengeance could strike *homo sacer* at any time, even in the form of murder by another person. In that case, the murderer would simply be viewed as an instrument of vengeance for the divinity in question. Brunnenmeister writes: "The sacer status has its basis in the much-attested belief that the gods would ... punish the evildoers themselves, when and how they wanted, and that no one, neither the state nor its bureaucrats nor priests nor individual citizens could preempt this punishment. No mortal could know which method the furious god would choose to lead his victim to inevitable ruin. Perhaps he would drive the guilty party to suicide with torments of all sort, perhaps he would bring him to his unexpected end in an accident, or let him slowly waste away, or perhaps the god would press a deadly weapon into human hands. He who slayed an accursed (*sacer*) man was considered innocent as soon as the conditions made clear that he, perhaps completely unwittingly, had been the instrument of divine vengeance. The thought that it was acceptable or even one's duty to help with human acts the offended god in his vengeful undertaking was foreign to the pious folk wisdom. The same dread which protected the property of the gods from harm also certainly kept reckless and malicious types from acting as worldly representatives of supernatural powers who had entrusted them to carry out punishments" (Brunnenmeister, *Das*

Tötungsverbrechen im altrömischen Recht, 152–153). What's more, Agamben claims that *homo sacer* isn't just excluded from the human order, but also the divine one, because he is unsuitable for sacrifice. That is a false conclusion; *homo sacer* cannot be sacrificed because he is *already* in the possession of the offended deity. Thus, the figure of *homo sacer* on which Agamben builds his theory of sovereignty proves to be a fiction that does not agree with historical fact.

94. The current focus on immunological discourse is also not a sign that contemporary society follows and immunological principle. When a paradigm itself is elevated as an object of reflection, this is often a sign that it is disappearing. Contemporary society has fallen into a pattern which deviates ever further from the principle of immunological defense. Immune reaction is only possible against the other or the foreign in the emphatic sense, but these are disappearing. The shift from the immunological age into the postimmunological age, in which the *same* prevails, is also connected to the process of globalization, which increasingly attempts to shed negativity in order to accelerate. The violence produced by the same cannot be averted immunologically. That is why it is more insidious than the violence of negativity.

95. Friedrich Nietzsche, "Nachgelassene Fragmente 1885–1887" in *Sämtliche Werke*, Vol 12 [new annotated edition] (Munich: dtv, 2005), 289–290.

96. Friedrich Nietzsche, *Thus Spoke Zarathustra*, trans. Adrian del Caro (Cambridge: Cambridge University Press, 2006), 32.

97. Agamben, *Homo Sacer*, 56.

98. Nietzsche's last man declares health to be the new goddess after the death of god: "[O]ne honors health. 'We invented happiness' say the last human beings, and they blink" (Nietzsche, *Thus Spoke Zarathustra*, 10).